Legitimacy and Commitment in the Military

Recent Titles in
Contributions in Military Studies

Arms Race Theory: Strategy and Structure of Behavior
Craig Etcheson

Strategic Impasse: Offense, Defense, and Deterrence Theory and Practice
Stephen J. Cimbala

Feeding the Bear: American Aid to the Soviet Union, 1941–1945
Hubert P. van Tuyll

Military Planning for the Defense of the United Kingdom, 1814–1870
Michael Stephen Partridge

The Hollow Army: How the U.S. Army Is Oversold and Undermanned
William Darryl Henderson

Reevaluating Major Naval Combatants of World War II
James J. Sadkovich, editor

The Culture of War: Invention and Early Development
Richard A. Gabriel

Prisoners, Diplomats, and the Great War: A Study in the Diplomacy of Captivity
Richard Berry Speed III

Military Crisis Management: U.S. Intervention in the Dominican Republic, 1965
Herbert G. Schoonmaker

The Persian Gulf War: Lessons for Strategy, Law, and Diplomacy
Christopher C. Joyner, editor

Where Eagles Land: Planning and Development of U.S. Army Airfields, 1910–1941
Jerold E. Brown

First Strike Stability: Deterrence after Containment
Stephen J. Cimbala

Legitimacy and Commitment in the Military

Edited by
Thomas C. Wyatt and Reuven Gal

CONTRIBUTIONS IN MILITARY STUDIES, NUMBER 100

Greenwood Press
New York • Westport, Connecticut • London

Library of Congress Cataloging-in-Publication Data

Legitimacy and commitment in the military / edited by Thomas C. Wyatt
and Reuven Gal.
  p.   cm. — (Contributions in military studies, ISSN 0883-6884 ;
  no. 100)
  Includes bibliographical references.
  ISBN 0-313-26815-0 (lib. bdg. : alk. paper)
  1. Sociology, Military. 2. Morale. 3. Military ethics.
  I. Wyatt, Thomas C. II. Gal, Reuven. III. Series.
  U21.5.L44   1990
  306.2'7—dc20   90-2944

British Library Cataloguing in Publication Data is available.

Library of Congress Catalog Card Number: 90-2944
ISBN: 0-313-26815-0
ISSN: 0883-6884

First published in 1990

Greenwood Press, 88 Post Road West, Westport, CT 06881
An imprint of Greenwood Publishing Group, Inc.

Printed in the United States of America

10 9 8 7 6 5 4 3 2 1

Contents

Figures and Tables

Introduction

The post–World War II wars are different wars. The military struggles in Algeria, Vietnam, Pakistan, Lebanon, the Falklands, and Grenada, to mention a few, were drastically different from the two world wars that occurred in the same century. Certainly the military confrontations that have taken place in Northern Ireland and in the *intifada* (the Palestinian uprising in the Israeli occupied territories) do not reflect traditional wars. These recent wars are characterized by issues of national consensus, home support, political debates, and moral argumentations and counterargumentations. When wars are evaluated by the number of demonstrations and the extent of alienation they provoke— when, instead of worrying about the number of casualties on the battlefield, governments start dealing with the number of draft-dodgers or conscientious objectors—these wars become different wars. In such wars, issues of legitimacy and commitment become the most essential components, not less, perhaps even more, than such issues as weapon systems, training, or tactics.

The military organizations of the last few decades are also different. These are armies that are prepared not only for war, but for peace, or peacekeeping missions. These armies may be occupied more in police, or constabulary, tasks than in combat manners. In some cases, these militaries comprise volunteers rather than conscripts. And many of these organizations move, gradually, from basically an institutional model to an occupational one—a trend that primarily involves changes in the sources of legitimacy and the nature of commitment.

The soldiers are different too. In a generation of *glastnost* and a growing resistance to the arms race, of idolized democracy and liberalism, of antimilitarism, antinationalism, and prohumanism, of youth becoming better educated and more sophisticated, combatants are no longer going to see themselves as compliantly executing orders. They will examine carefully the sources of the military legitimation before furnishing the unconditional commitment that is the backbone of the military fighting spirit.

These are the basic assumptions of this book. In the changing world of the 1990s there are still some basic prerequisites underlying the armed forces. What all military activities—whether combat or constabulary—have in common are human values. No military organization can operate without legitimacy. And no troops will fight without commitment.

This book looks at the issues of legitimacy and commitment in the military not as they have been understood in past wars. It does not idly preach military ethics. The eleven chapters incorporated in this volume, written by a group of leading behavioral scientists, analyze critically current fault lines and future trends in this area. The contributors represent a wide scope of disciplines—psychology, sociology, history, philosophy, anthropology, and military studies—and a variety of nations and perspectives. As a whole, this volume provides an essential collection for the military student: the scholar, the soldier, and the leader.

PART I

Theoretical Issues: Values, Legitimacy, and Commitment

The first part of this book deals with some of the theoretical puzzles that face us whenever we deal with the combination of military ethics and moral values. Among the necessary concepts required to deal with this puzzle are those of legitimacy and commitment. Although legitimacy stems from the legal-ethical arenas and commitment refers to the organizational-motivational aspects of behavior, they intersect in the fields of the military profession and political decision making.

The first chapter considers the various types of military legitimacy—the legitimacy of waging a war and the legitimacy of war conduct. The author, a military psychologist and a veteran of several wars between Israel and the Arab states, approaches the issues from both an historical perspective and his own experience. In the course of attempting to delineate the ambiguous criteria for "just" wars and for legitimate war methods, the complexity of this issue becomes very apparent. It is exactly this complexity and ambiguity that makes, in Reuven Gal's opinion, commitment—rather than obedience—the ultimate mode of military compliance.

Hillel Levine, an historian and a sociologist, provides an historical perspective of the issue, from medieval times through the Nuremberg trials, to the My Lai incident, and the future battlefield. This chapter provides another important distinction—that between the specific legitimation of certain acts, including acts based on personal commitment, and the more universal legitimacy of the same acts, in light of their ethical and moral virtues.

The sociological-ethical perspective, theoretical and empirical, is provided by Donald L. Lang. The author, who has long taught officer cadets in the Canadian Military Academy, analyzes the roles of values, commitment, and legitimacy within an organizational context, particularly the military organization. At the same time, he incorporates analyses of related issues, such as motivation, freedom of choice, and role behavior. According to Lang, legitimacy resides solely in the soldier's role, as a member of the military organization, whereas his commitment is essentially a conscious, solely subjective, process. Deriving again from his own research, Lang concludes that the individual's (in this case, the soldier's) value system is the linchpin between commitment and legitimacy.

The last contributor in this section, Charles A. Cotton, is also a Canadian scholar and a soldier. "Sandy" Cotton asserts that the issue of military commitment has plagued him for many years. Based on his own observations, as well as on a large-scale study he has conducted, he concludes, unequivocally, that "commitment is the sine qua non of effectiveness in volunteer military systems." He also claims that there are dangers, difficulties, and demands in this area. Although the military must develop, feed, and set the limits to the commitments of its members, it must also engage itself in a constant "institutional introspection" in regard to its tenets and beliefs.

Thus, the four chapters that open this volume lay the ground for a better understanding of the relationships among commitment, legitimacy, values, and other related concepts. They also illuminate the intricacy, intangibility, and abstruseness that characterize these terms. Even though such characteristics are almost the antonyms of the daily martial vocabulary, it is evident from these chapters that the military profession depends critically on these foundations.

1

Limits of Military Legitimacy and Its Relation to Military Commitment

Reuven Gal

Legitimacy, commitment, and moral values—all are key terms in the area of military ethics.[1] The term military ethics itself would be called by some an oxymoron—what does the military have to do with ethics? After all, the ultimate function of every military organization is to execute collective violence in the service of social goals. Our soldiers are expected to perform—with great decisiveness—those very destructive actions that we have always preached to them never to do. It is because of this moral dilemma that the military depends so critically on such concepts as military ethics, commitment, and legitimacy.

Strangely enough, we do not find that much involvement with ethics and its related concepts with regard to other occupations that are relatively close to the military profession. Very rarely does one find any references to firemen's ethics, fishermen's ethics, or pilots' ethics—to mention only three of those combat-like professions. Military ethics, on the other hand, is a wide-spread issue for both military professionals and military students. Furthermore, military leaders—perhaps more than any other professionals—are expected to demonstrate not only outstanding skills and professional competence, but also such intangible qualities as honesty, loyalty, commitment, courage, and, above all, moral integrity. Why?

There are two main reasons for this extra emphasis on military ethics. First, the military profession must be morally sound and operate by strict ethical rules because it is the only institutionalized profession that deals with the most delicate aspects of human beings—life and death.

For those who have been authorized by their society to employ vast lethal instruments aimed to take, or save, other humans' lives, loyalty, honesty, and moral integrity are not just terms that describe characteristics that are nice to have; they are a vital necessity for the military profession. One other profession in which ethics frequently receive emphasis is medicine. Indeed, doctors too deal with life and death. However, whereas medicine is devoted to the saving of human lives, normally on an individual basis, the military is engaged in both saving lives and causing death, normally en masse.

Second, the military profession is not just an occupation. Neither is it engaged only in training and operations. For most Western societies the military has a symbolic function: its members—officers and soldiers alike—represent cultural and societal values. The armed forces of a nation are perceived as the guarantee of the continual existence of that nation and its government which, in turn, provides individual protection and a structure of law.[2] Ethical behavior, thus, is for the military not just an external decoration. It is essential, authentic, and binding.

The issue of military legitimacy—the legitimacy of wars and the legitimacy of war conduct—is perhaps the most central issue within the arena of military ethics.[3] The perception and interpretation of legitimacy by the soldier is, at times, the ultimate test of his honesty, loyalty, and moral integrity.

Furthermore, the military institute itself has become, in recent years, a target for critical inquiries regarding its own perception and interpretation of military legitimacy. Such critics have become more salient in the last two decades for several reasons: the increasing dependence on nuclear weaponry, the growing public attitude against any military employment for political goals, the replacement of the draft by volunteer personnel, the growing burden that military expenses are waging on a nation's GNP, the repeated scandals involving arms procurements and weapon sales, and the increasing involvement of armed forces in peacekeeping and other nations' affairs (as opposed to war-related and home-protection involvements). These trends and changes, among others, have made the legitimacy issue a growing concern, not so much to the mere existence of the military institution, but particularly with regard to various decisions made by the military.

For the genuine pacifist the question of war legitimacy does not exist at all. There are no legitimate wars. Period. But for the military professional it is a sobering question. More precisely, there are two separate questions. The first question concerns the legitimacy of war (*jus ad bellum*); that is, when, under what conditions, and in what circumstances a war is legitimate. The second question is that of legitimacy in war (*jus in bello*); in other words, once a war has been declared, what methods and which means are legitimate in conducting the war?

In regard to the first question, it has been long phrased as the question of just and unjust wars. Interestingly enough, this phrase was first coined (and discussed) by theologists and philosophers, not by warriors. St. Augustine, in the fourth century, is probably one of the earliest thinkers to deal with the issue. Later, in the thirteenth century, it was St. Thomas Aquinas, the Italian theologian, who further developed the subject. Aquinas suggested three criteria to distinguish between just (i.e., legitimate) and unjust wars. First, was the war declared by a legitimate authority? Second, did the war break out for just causes? Third, what was the intention? To paraphrase St. Thomas, those who wage wars justly—[can] have [only] peace as the object of their intention.

On the face of it, these three clear, straightforward criteria—authority, cause, and intention—can be used to test the legitimacy of war. On the other hand, they are not that clear and simple. Each one of these criteria faces serious difficulties, both logical and epistemological.

For example, how is it possible to determine the legitimacy of a war as contingent upon the legitimacy of the authority? One of the very definitions of political authority is its ability to legitimate wars. This leads us to a confusing tautology. Furthermore, using the test of cause, we confront yet another logical dilemma. Although it is true that modern politics have accepted only direct aggression or self-defense as just causes for wars, this has created the paradox of going to war in order to avoid war.

But the most difficult of these problems is the question of whose decision it is: Who decides what is a legitimate authority? Who decides what are just causes? Who decides whether the intentions are right or not? The answers to these questions are anything but objective. "All symbolic universes and all legitimations are human products; their existence has its base in the lives of concrete individuals and has no empirical status apart from these lives."[4] Even the Holocaust, or any other brutal military operation, can be presented, by way of an intellectual exercise, as a legitimate war by applying these three criteria.

The same difficulties apply to the second issue—that of legitimacy in war, the legitimacy of war conduct. Here the common criteria (other than the existing agreements regarding the treatment of POWs and wounded soldiers) require that the war not harm the innocents, that the means used will be proportional, that the war methods do not deviate from agreed standards, and so on.

These criteria instigate more questions than provide answers. For example, if a legitimate conduct of war is not to harm the innocents, the question becomes who are the innocents? Were the British citizens who endured the World War II blitz innocents? Were the German citizens of Dresden or Berlin innocents? No one among the Allies, in February 1945, considered the massive air-attack that left more than 60,000 innocent dead in the ruins of Dresden to be illegitimate. When the Israelis invaded Lebanon in 1983 in search of the PLO terrorists, they declared that they would not harm the innocents; did that make any sense after the Palestinian guerillas had hidden deliberately in civilian houses, hospitals, and schools? Is it at all possible, in today's civil wars, to distinguish between the innocent and the noninnocent? What about those who collaborate and support but do not directly fight—are they innocent?

The same questions arise with regard to war methods. Does the criterion of agreed standard apply more justifiably to our modern—albeit conventional—weapon systems, with their tremendous lethal effect, than it does to, say, chemical weapons?

And suppose that lethal chemical warheads will be utilized meticulously only against fighting soldiers in uniforms—does that make them legitimate? These and others are oppressing questions. The discussion about legitimacy—both of war and in war—does not provide guidelines and rules of thumb; it evokes doubts and questions. But this is good. Military ethics cannot be dictated by simple rules or guidelines; instead, they are generated, maintained, and further developed by continuously questioning, by raising doubts, by examining changing conditions, and by searching for new solutions.

Following World War II, the international Law Commission, instigated by the UN, defined seven principles governing the acts of individuals in war. One of these principles states that the fact that a person acted on the orders of his government or a superior does not relieve him from responsibility under international law, *provided a moral choice was in fact open to him*. This is an excellent example of an oppressing question that might preoccupy a combat soldier at any moment: Is, in fact, a moral choice open to him in any given situation?

Such an approach to military ethics and to the issue of legitimacy leads the way to commitment as a mode of military compliance and a source of combat motivation. Where mere obedience to government or superior does not relieve the combatant from his own responsibility, the only alternative is personal commitment. Commitment is characterized as a sense of duty that originates from within. Based on a complex network of personal beliefs, self-convictions, and inner decisions, it is initially generated by recognition of a need and by the power of related values and norms and is motivated further by the sense of justified goals. Most typically, it allows for doubts and it facilitates reexamination, even resistance.[5]

Only a sense of duty that stems from one's beliefs, guided by continuous reexamination of internalized goals, can suggest solutions to questions about the legitimacy of one's actions.

NOTES

1. James Brown and Michael J. Collins, eds., *Military Ethics and Professionalism: A Collection of Essays* (Fort McNair, Washington, D.C.: Na-

tional Defense University Press, 1981); Richard A. Gabriel, *To Serve with Honor* (Westport, Conn.: Greenwood Press, 1982); Morris Janowitz, *The Professional Soldier* (New York: The Free Press, 1971); and Malham M. Wakin, ed., *War, Morality, and the Military Profession* (Boulder, Colo.: Westview Press, 1979).

2. Max Weber, *The Theory of Social and Economic Organization*, trans. A. M. Henderson and T. Parsons (New York: The Free Press, 1964).

3. Gwyn Harries-Jenkins and Jacques vanDoorn, eds., *The Military and the Problem of Legitimacy* (Beverly Hills, Calif.: Sage Publications, 1976).

4. Peter L. Berger and Thomas Luckman, *The Social Construction of Reality* (New York: Doubleday, 1966), p. 118.

5. Reuven Gal, "Commitment and Obedience in the Military: An Israeli Case Study," *Armed Forces and Society* 11, no. 4 (Summer 1985), pp. 553–64.

2

Between Social Legitimation and Moral Legitimacy in Military Commitment

Hillel Levine

The connections postulated to exist between legitimacy and commitment are by no means new.[1] That there will be a greater commitment to the goals of the state, particularly those undertaken in its war efforts, if the citizen can identify with those goals and justify them is at the foundation of diverse political philosophies. More recently, the link between legitimacy and commitment has received added support from experimental social psychological data.[2] What poses new and vexing problems, however, are the precarious sources of that legitimacy.

Models of civic virtue, previewed in the classical period, during the Renaissance, and in revolutionary England, include the role and detail the duties of the citizen-soldier.[3] Mercenaries, soldiers of fortune, and armed peasants were always looked upon with suspicion for reasons other than their questionable reliability. Industrialization and the application of new technologies to agriculture increased the manpower and resources available for the developing centralized states to maintain standing armies and to wage war. At the same time, higher literacy and political consciousness among soldiers, as illustrated by the French troops recruited and trained during the French Revolution and the Napoleonic wars, pointed to the military value of commitment based upon the soldiers' belief in the legitimacy of their actions and cause. Modern military scientists, from the nineteenth century on, questioned the usefulness of mindless soldiers placed along lines as bowling pins or dispatched as cannon fodder, even when limitless numbers of recruits were seemingly available to replenish the battlefield and heavy personnel losses could be justified in the political arena back home. Commitment, it was observed, could certainly be strengthened, if only temporarily, by the soldiers' high morale, induced often by little more than booty, wild sprees, and rest and recreation. But the scientific management of war required a more sustained commitment grounded in attitudes other than self-interest and passions other than excitement. The suffering and danger that soldiers endured needed to be bolstered in principle and rewarded by the dispensation of good conscience. Optimal performance on all levels of military operation required a pervasive belief in the legitimacy of what was to be done rather than the mere obedience to orders and the performance of duties in good spirits.

It is precisely here that our problem begins because the period—at least in the West—during which the military organization went through the most significant modernization and bureaucratization corresponded with the period in which the specific institutions that in the past, had provided the legitimations for war were in decline. Consequently, the ultimate burden of discerning legitimacy was shifted to some uncertain seat of conscience and to the personal thoughts of the individual. Yet, at the very moment when the individual became responsible to deal with questions of legitimacy, the individual's ability to make a careful assessment of important issues rather than simply to conform with the actions of others or take directives from superiors increasingly was called into question. When the consensus developed that it is imperative—not only for the soldier but also the citizen—to disobey orders that may be legal within a particular system but are otherwise immoral and when this principle became firmly ensconced in international law, the very capacity of individuals to think and to act responsibly and independently was challenged.

Religion has served as the traditional arbiter of the notions of a just war.[4] Religions provided more than the motivating ideas for the holy community to go forth in battle and the rituals to protect the bodies and raise the morale of the sacred warriors; the more reflective aspects of religion itself provided nuanced arguments by which violence could be legitimated. In the modern military organizations of most Western nations, religion has been relegated to the tasks of sprinkling a bit of holy water here and there and of personal ministry to the troops by uniformed chaplains who mostly confine their religious services to the confessional and do not promote the didactic or ethical dimensions of their religion, at least in regard to questions regarding the legitimacy of military activities. The universal church has been assumed, of course, by the modern state, to be eminently suited to dispense justifications for war because of its power, its influence on the media of communications and education, and its claims to an amoral *raison d'état*. In recent years, however, transnational ideologies, with their own means for indoctrination, have competed with the state as the matrix of legitimacy. Moreover, not only has the promulgation of ultimate legitimacy by the state been questioned, but skeptical attitudes toward this prerogative have been translated into law.

It is in this regard that the Nuremberg trials represent an important watershed.[5] Those trials, as is now well known, were not prompted primarily by some dramatic expansion of the inner rationality of law to meet new exigencies. The statesmen, who at the height of battle reflected upon some international tribunal to take place at the successful conclusion of the war, were concerned on the one hand to deter the Nazis from certain acts and on the other hand to bolster the morale of the troops by making early pronouncements upon the fate of "the forces of darkness." As the successful outcome of the war for the Allies became assured and the efforts began to translate vague pronouncements into formal arrangements, the divergent positions of the war leaders emerged. Winston Churchill and Joseph Stalin were in disagreement. Stalin was most insistent upon trying war criminals. Churchill, at this time, was not concerned with formal legality, supposing that at the proper moment it would be sufficient to dispatch from back alleys those who were obviously guilty. He was most concerned, however, not to allow Stalin the show trials for which the Communist regimes had become infamous. Franklin D. Roosevelt, upholding the principle of law, resolved the conflict leading to the planning of an international tribunal.

The earliest formulation by the planners of the Nuremberg trials of the universally regarded and authoritative principles upon which the Nazis could be tried included crimes against peace, war crimes, and crimes against humanity. Questions of the authority of the state in defining what was legitimate, at that time, it was thought, would have to be sidestepped. As the U.S. Supreme Court Justice Robert Jackson put it, "Unless we have a war connection, I would think that we have no bases for dealing with the atrocities committed inside of Germany under German law." As the magnitude of human suffering caused by the Nazis came to be more fully confronted, however, and as the vision of a new order became more necessary, the enthusiasm to provide a new legal base increased. This enthusiasm is recorded in the statements of some of the architects of the tribunal. For example, an American planner, Lieutenant Colonel Murray Bernays, said, "Not to try these beasts would be to miss the educational and therapeutic opportunity of our generation. That they must be tried not only for their specific aims but for the bestiality from which these crimes sprang." By the time the tribunal actually began, Jackson shared the enthusiasm of the less cautious jurists, saying that "the time has come for the law to leap and step forward."

The visions of Nuremberg's planners for a permanent international criminal tribunal and a law that would be internationally enforceable have not come to fruition. Nevertheless, the law did "leap forward" in the sense that it gave the most authoritative recognition to the principle that the sovereign nation-state, however legitimate it might be in formal terms, cannot abrogate its responsibilities to higher laws that its citizens must obey. The obedience to superior orders that are legal in any particular context but are immoral in relation to some higher law is, at best, a mitigating factor. The historical processes whereby the locus of moral discernment was shifted to the individual was thus confirmed by law. Moreover, the very parameters of those responsible for criminal acts were expanded to include not only the actual perpetrators but also the policymakers. Generals, cabinet members, and civilians, including industrialists—not ordinary soldiers or low-ranking officers—were the ones who were put on trial first. The counterdefense to superior orders—the claims made by high-level officials that they had no knowledge of, and therefore were not responsible for, what took place in the field—was summarily rejected, particularly in the Tokyo war tribunal of General Yamashita. General Douglas MacArthur found no extenuating circumstances in the impaired communication brought about among the Japanese forces during their retreat which, as the defense claimed for General Yamashita, made him unaware of what was taking place. The legal test for responsibility was to be not actual knowledge but assumed knowledge.[6]

The legacy of Nuremberg, therefore, leads us to demand more at the very moment that we are prepared to expect less of soldiers or, for that matter, officers and policymakers in regard to their abilities to legitimate their actions in terms that have anything to do with philosophical notions of legitimacy, distinguishing as they would between good and evil. History has provided us with a long and tragic record of the devices used by people to deceive themselves and others. The social sciences have enabled us to examine the imaginative capacities of people to provide self-serving rationalizations of their actions and to project motives, unacceptable to themselves, onto others. Vast cultural resources—the stuff out of which come violent myths and frightening nightmares—stand at the disposal of those who would want to "malign" others.[7] Language itself from this perspective becomes the chief promulgator of deceptions, shielding with euphemism and bureaucratic jargon the individual who is obligated to make independent moral evaluations from the horrors to which that individual's actions might lead. Propaganda relates to legitimacy as high morale does to commitment—as a somewhat necessary but altogether insufficient cause. Technologies and indoctrination that dehumanize the enemy and modes of military organization that devalue the individual, reducing the soldier's sense of personal agency and responsibility, facilitate violence. Studies of behavior under stress point to increased impulsiveness; research on group pressures shows the influence of the group to impair the judgment of individuals. The incremental errors which stem from the needs of individuals to maintain a sense of their own invulnerability and the just world in which they live make individuals wholly unreliable sources of detached philosophical analysis and arbiters of legitimacy, both as actors and as observers.[8]

Inadequate senses of causality, naive notions of justice, and poor comprehension of, or even total ignorance of, established codes of law raise serious questions about the ability of soldiers, particularly under battle conditions, to determine what is legitimate, even in democracies posited upon the assumption that individuals are best able to reflect upon and represent their own true interests.

This limited capacity of individuals to provide legitimations for their commitment that have anything to do with legitimacy in a philosophical sense was illustrated laconically and poignantly in Lieutenant Calley's explanation during his court martial for atrocities perpetrated at My Lai: "I didn't discriminate between individuals, Sir. They were all the enemy, they were all to be destroyed, Sir."[9] This soldier's reality was not touched by the millennia of doctrines on just war, by international tribunals, and by the Nuremberg idea, as lofty as all of these might be. His was the reality of body counts, of Zippo raids, and of free-fire zones—efforts to "pacify the countryside." This was a reality that was defined for him as much by civilian policymakers, military planners, and the officers who gave him his orders as it was by his lack of moral discernment, this poor perception of the political realities of rural Vietnam, and his accurate sense of overwhelming danger. The socially provided legitimations of Lieutenant Calley, by which he sought to justify his actions to himself and to others, did not outweigh the expectations of the court to demand of him commitment based on some principled notion of legitimacy. Lieutenant Calley was held responsible for his actions. Other courts provided by a democracy in which the actions of individuals are assessed, such as the media and public opinion, seemed to be more equivocal in their expectations of Calley.[10] In a rather extraordinary act—one which did not illustrate the best of democratic procedure—a president expressed his opinion and intervened procedurally. The attention received by this trial illustrates the difficulty in achieving consensus between the extreme positions of "everyone is guilty" and "no one is ultimately responsible."

The Vietnam War opened these questions in a painful way, and the protracted debate has still not clarified many of the issues. The Peers Commission Report, made public in 1974, in the "Findings and Recommendations," paragraph IE, points to the tragic discrepancy between the law on the books and the law in practice: "In 1968, the then existing policies and directives at every level of command expressed a clear intent regarding the proper treatment and safeguarding of noncombatants, the handling of prisoners of war, and minimizing the destruction of private property."[11] It goes on to point out how, nevertheless, the soldiers in the Eleventh Brigade who were investigated were not trained adequately in regard to their responsibilities to disobey any orders received from superiors that were illegal and to report war crimes. The procedures were not spelled out, and the soldiers had no clear sense of the provision of the Geneva Convention in the handling and treatment of prisoners of war and the treatment and safeguarding of noncombatants. The author of the report, in his section on "Omissions and Commissions by Individuals" presents a detailed catalogue of accusations against those who were related to My Lai from the highest to the lowest level. Although this commission report underscores the importance of bridging the gap between the law on the books and the law in the field, between the world of regulations and the soldier's realities, it provides no program to fill in the deficiencies in training and the ambiguities in the directives that it catalogues.

The military services have continued the agonizing work of self-scrutiny begun in this commission report in an effort to learn the lessons of Vietnam. Few professions have undertaken such thorough self-scrutiny as the military. The Army War College Study of Military Professionalism of 1971, the study of Lieutenant Melville Drisko in 1977, the Squadron Officers Study of 1978—all point to patterns of variances between ideal and actual standards and all call for a more intensive concentration on military ethics on different levels of military training. Such popular additions—Field Manual number 27–2, "Your Conduct in Combat under the Law of War," issued in November 1984—try to adumbrate new foundations to ensure the connections between the legitimations that soldiers will provide for their actions and legitimacy.

A protracted in-house debate has taken place over the need for and the utility of a new code of military ethics. Those who recognize the need for a formalized code that would guide professional behavior of members of the military argue that it would strengthen the trust and confidence between civilians and the military profession, that it would shape the character of the members of the military, and, by establishing standards of honor and sacrifice, it would provide a sense of community based upon shared obligations. The opponents to the formalization of such a code question whether ethics can be learned or enforced by external authority and express concern lest an explicit code establish a minimal standard and become a poor substitute for ethical judgment in the infinite and discretionary situations requiring ethical analysis of diverse possibilities for action.[12]

But the advocates of both extreme positions in this argument may be missing the essential point: Under battle conditions, making moral distinctions, however explicit the ethical principles have been made, is difficult. Moreover, soldiers have well-developed capacities to legitimate their actions without necessary recourse to principles of legitimacy. To encourage military planners and soldiers to protect civilian populations as far as possible, to fight effectively but to avoid inflicting cruelty, to take prisoners of war and to act honorably if taken as a prisoner of war, to disobey legal but immoral orders from superiors, and to pass information up through the hierarchy on breaches of regulation or on conditions inadequately perceived by decision makers—all of these behaviors require training in specific and well-defined procedures as well as indoctrination in principles. And, although a sense of honor, professionalism, and decency are quite necessary for ethical behavior, the modes of behavior that are sought require training and the rewards should derive from the satisfaction of following procedure in an engaged manner. Both those who are prepared to rely on some vague sense of soldier's honor and those who believe in draftsmanship may be missing important opportunities to provide ideas for new procedures and institutions based on the lessons learned from

the battlefield, from the activities of POWs, and from the ago-
nized discussions of terrorized populations in Nazi ghettos. And
although the social sciences have no claim to be the new and
ultimate arbiters of right and wrong and dispensers of legitimacy, far too often, having discredited themselves in public
policy and in courts of law, there is room for the collaboration
of social scientists, organizational theorists, and ethicists in providing counterstrategies to what we know about the forces that
impair human judgment.[13]

An example of this can be seen in the studies of poor decision
making in groups where, as has been indicated, the cogency of
arguments and the value of specific bits of information are often
unduly influenced by the social position of individuals contributing to the decision-making process. This "groupthink" can be
neutralized, first by awareness of the problem and second by
the use of simple devices such as the devil's advocate.[14] Techniques of gaming and simulation, effectively used in training of
all sorts, could now be used to bridge the disparate realities of
policy-making, military training, and actual military operations.
The stressful and dangerous conditions under which prisoners
of war must be taken, for example, call for careful training as
an integral part of war games and the allocation of specific resources such as manpower and equipment, in addition to codes
and lectures, if soldiers are to understand that it really is important to take POWs rather than to deal with them at five paces
from the rear.[15] Disobedience of the illegal orders of superiors
must be translated carefully into procedures and bolstered by
incentives and protection such as the institutionalization of om-
budsmen if this responsibility of soldiers is to be taken seriously
and, at the same time, not undermine legitimate authority. Although the complexities of modern warfare and the remoteness
between combatants in the electronic battlefield do not make
the environment most conducive to rule governance, there are
modes of thinking and well-defined procedures that can enable
soldiers who are neither professional philosophers nor lawyers
to have a sense that they know what is and what is not legitimate
and to provide soldiers on all levels of the military hierarchy
with a sense that following orders does not necessarily make
them cogs on the wheel. Neither the army of automatons—

value-free technicians applying military skills in a moral vacuum because they are ordered to do so by the state—nor the *jihad*—the masses of true believers totally ideologized—exhaust all of the possibilities. In this regard, the officer who sets a moral example is most important. The cynicism engendered by war-weary officers toward their soldiers in training, between the law on the books and the "war is hell" realities of the battlefield, can and has subverted the best planned programs in military ethics.

Rules are not amulets; they have no magical powers. The army must tend to the physical as well as the moral dangers of soldiering, taking men into battle and returning them to society with their respect for life and their capacity to make moral choices unimpaired. The commitment of soldiers who were and will be citizens again must be strengthened through legitimations that are not bereft of legitimacy. The memorization of moral codes or legal conventions will not provide soldiers with the guidance and the inspiration needed to protect them from succumbing to savagery. This is particularly true when precombat training is contrasted to battlefield conditions and life experiences that are assigned an ultimately authoritative and reliably practical mandate of their own. The day-to-day operations, the procedures with which there is the greatest familiarity, must be suffused with issues derived from legitimacy. Training and accounting for military ethics must be deep within the military organization.

The military has difficult problems in balancing between obedience to authority and independent moral judgment; between protecting the morale and camaraderie of the group and the need to train soldiers who can disobey an unlawful order with good judgment and courage and will pass important information on conditions and activities back up the hierarchy so that they can have an impact on the policymakers and on the opinion of the citizens who are ultimately responsible and in whose name the violence is being perpetrated for a higher cause. These problems are difficult, indeed, but they lend themselves to some conceptual and technical remedies. Emphasizing the philosophical dimensions over and above all else can become an unintended mode of obfuscation.

NOTES

1. See K.M. Waltz, *Man, the State and War: A Theoretical Analysis* (New York, 1959), and Michael Walzer, *Just and Unjust Wars* (New York, 1977).

2. Herbert Kelman, "Patterns of Personal Involvement in the National System: A Social Psychology Analysis of Political Legitimacy," in *International Politics and Foreign Policy*, ed. James Rosenau (New York, 1969).

3. J.G.A. Pocock, *The Machiavellian Moment* (Princeton, 1975); "Cambridge Paradigms and Scotch Philosophers: A Study of the Relations between the Civic Humanist and the Civil Jurisprudential Interpretation of Eighteenth Century Thought," in *Wealth and Virtue*, ed. I. Hont and M. Ignatieff (New York, 1984).

4. James Johnson, *Ideology, Reason and the Limitations of War: Religious and Secular Concepts, 1200–1740* (Princeton, N.J., 1975).

5. Telford Taylor, *Nuremberg and Vietnam: An American Tragedy* (Chicago, 1970).

6. This received fuller elaboration and formalization as a principle of indirect responsibility in the Kahan Commission Report following the Beirut massacres in September 1982. See *The Beirut Massacre: The Complete Kahan Commission Report* (New York, 1983), pp. 56–63.

7. Hillel Levine, "On the Debanalization of Evil," in *Sociology and Human Destiny*, ed. G. Baum (New York, 1980).

8. Irving Janis, *Stress and Frustration* (New York, 1971); Fritz Heider, "Social Perceptions and Phenomenal Causality," *Psychological Review* 51 (1944), pp. 358–73; and Lee Ross, *Cognitive Theories in Social Psychology: Papers from Advances in Experimental Psychology*, ed. Leonard Berkowitz (New York, 1978), pp. 338–43.

9. Joseph Goldstein, Burke Marshall, and Jack Schwartz, *The My Lai Massacre and Its Cover-Up: Beyond the Reach of Law* (New York, 1976), p. 9.

10. Lee Lawrence and Herbert Kelman, "Reactions to the Calley Trial: Class and Political Authority," *Worldview* 16, no. 6 (June 1973), pp. 34–40.

11. Goldstein, Marshall, and Schwartz, *My Lai Massacre*, p. 319.

12. Richard Gabriel, *To Serve with Honor: A Treatise on Military Ethics and the Way of the Soldier* (Westport, Conn., 1982), pp. 119–49.

13. For a balanced position on models of personal responsibility based on law and on social science knowledge, see Stephen Morse, "Crazy Behavior, Morals and Science: An Analysis of Mental Health Law," *Southern California Law Review* 51, no. 4 (May 1978), pp. 561–64.

14. Irving Janis, *Groupthink* (Boston, 1982).

15. Goldstein, Marshall, and Schwartz, *My Lai Massacre*, pp. 8–9.

3

Values: The Ultimate Determinants of Commitment and Legitimacy

Donald L. Lang

The purpose of this chapter is to argue that values are the final arbiter of a soldier's commitment and his legitimacy to act. The arguments proceed from Hodgkinson's analysis of values in an organizational context and the author's research investigating the commitment of individuals to organizations.[1]

The primary issues are values, organizational commitment, motivation, freedom of choice (will), and roles. The findings of the author's research are presented, followed by conclusions and implications for organizational behavior.

For the purposes of this chapter, organizational commitment is defined as the manifestation of the congruency between individual and organizational value systems, moderated by the effects of role occupancy. This definition implies that organizational commitment is essentially a conscious, value-based process. Legitimacy is used in the sense given by Katz and Kahn.[2] It involves formal rules for behavior in accordance with organizational directives, accepted beliefs about proper procedure, and generally held beliefs about matters of right and wrong.

PRIMARY ISSUES

Values

In his comprehensive review of the literature on values, Girdon concludes that there is little consensus about the meaning of the term value.[3]

The inability of social scientists to achieve a sense of closure on values as a researchable variable is not a consequence of the scientific method. Aristotle had the same problem: The man of practical wisdom (*phronimos*) is the ultimate sanction in ethical behavior, but the criterion for what is good is the good man (*spoudaios*).[4]

Concern about values in an organizational context may be said to have begun with Barnard's "moral complexity."[5] Yet many contemporary texts on organizational behavior give scant attention to the subject, even though the problem has been identified for many years.[6] In 1963, McMurray, in commenting on the matter of "unreasonableness" in interpersonal relations in industry, acknowledges the parts played by poor communications, lack of knowledge, and poor management styles, but he asserts that value conflict is the root of the problem.[7]

Even systems analysts express concern about values in their genre of work.[8] Others are outright pessimistic about delineating values as a researchable variable.[9]

The problem is philosophical, not methodological. Researchers with a logical, positivist perspective are forced to take an ethically neutered perspective of man. Simon is the exponent in organizational behavior; Skinner in a general behavioral sense, typified by Fodor's claim that computer software capable of making ethical judgments is near at hand.[10] Hodgkinson presents a fundamentally different philosophical perspective, essentially an Aristotelian-Thomistic viewpoint, as is Barnard's. Value is interpreted as rationally based and will dependent. Animals do not have values. Values are principles that guide human acts (as distinct from acts of man), a position consistent with Hodgkinson, Kluckhohn, and Rokeach but inconsistent with some leading organizational theorists; for example, Vroom, who makes no essential distinction between man and animals, and

Locke, who views values as a biological function. This is instinctualism.[11]

Hodgkinson postulates three logically distinct types of value-based behavior: transrational values, rational values, and subrational values. Transrational values (type I) are based on faith and will. Individuals behave the way they do because they believe in what they are doing. Rational values are either clearly logic based (type IIA) or consensual based (type IIB). Individuals behave the way they do because of concern about the consequences of their activities, or because others behave that way. Subrational values (type III) are pleasure based. Individuals behave the way they do because they like it. Since pure types are unlikely to be found in reality (Weber),[12] it is reasonable to expect that combinations of these value types will guide individual behavior. In this context, Hodgkinson postulates that they are hierarchically ordered: type I values influence type II values and type III values, and type II values influence type III values.

Organizational Commitment

The literature on organizational commitment is presented from four perspectives: Barnardian influence, typologies, empirical studies, and models.

1. Barnard's 1938 classical work, *The Functions of the Executive*, identified several substantive concepts which continue to guide current research investigating the commitment of individuals to organizations, usually referred to as organizational commitment. *Equilibrium*—what one gives to an organization and expects in return—is found in Burns' transactional leadership, Jacobs' social exchange, Schien's psychological contract, and Simon's inducements-contributions.[13] They all represent quid pro quo. *Identification*, his notion of willingness, is Moskos' criterion of institutional type organizations and is integral to the work of Mowday, Porter, and Steers.[14] *Nomothesis-idiography*, his dual personality, the distinction between person-as-individual and person-as-organization-member, is central to the work of Getzels and Guba[15] and Hodgkinson. But Barnard's most significant concept is *communion*: the "glue" of brotherhood and comrade-

ship. This is contained in the meanings of ethos and cohesion by Cotton, Gabriel, and Moskos.[16]

2. Typological research is grounded in Weber's notion of "ideal construct" as a legitimate epistemological process. Relevant examples are Cotton's "soldier," "ambivalent," and "civilian"; Etzioni's normative (moral), calculative, and coercive types of commitment; Kanter's continuous, cohesion, and control types; and Hall and Schneider's six types.[17]

3. Two schools of thought guide current empirical research investigating organizational commitment. The attitudinal school, represented mainly by Porter and his associates, Mowday and Steers, view commitment as an attitude.[18] It is identification with and involvement in a particular organization. It is characterized by belief in and acceptance of the goals and values of the organization, a willingness to exert extra effort on behalf of the organization, and a strong desire to retain membership. The behavioral school, represented by Staw and Salancik,[19] view commitment as a series of behaviors which "bind" the individual to the organization, as a result of "investments." These investments refer to psychological states (e.g., ego involvement) and physical states (e.g., time), which, prior to organizational involvement, are neutral but, subsequent to involvement, take on another dimension—an investment of psychological energy and time which makes it difficult or painful for the individual to withdraw. Hence the individual becomes bound to the organization. Mowday, Porter, and Steers now maintain that both approaches are necessary to explain organizational commitment, where attitudes and behaviors reinforce each other.

This type of research was initially directed toward the development of scales to measure commitment.[20] Subsequent research emphasized Steers' notion of the antecedents and consequences of commitment.[21] Antecedents refer to personal characteristics (e.g., age, education), role-related characteristics (e.g., challenging job), structural characteristics (e.g., size of organization), and work experience characteristics (e.g., feeling important). Consequences of commitment include absenteeism and attrition. Research on this work has been succinctly summarized by Mowday, Porter, and Steers.[22] As data have accumulated, a basic typology of what could be called moral and calculative commitment has emerged,[23] which has theoretical support in earlier organizational theory[24] and in philosophy.[25]

Recent research deals with the relationship between commitment and quality circles,[26] central life interest, age and profession,[27] leadership,[28] and conflict.[29]

Research which could be included here is that undertaken by Stahl, McNichols, and Manley[30] who, like empirical referees in the Moskos-Janowitz debate, have provided data that show that military personnel can espouse both institutional and organizational value systems.[31]

4. Models illustrate researchers' attempts to integrate key concepts, even though opinions differ as to how they are to be used.[32] The model by Stevens, Beyer, and Trice incorporates the seminal work of Kahn et al.,[33] and exchange theory. Personal attributes, role-related factors, and organizational factors impact upon the individual's perceived role. The individual then undergoes an exchange/evaluation process which leads to role enactment. In Staw's model, commitment is the outcome of the integration of introspective and prospective rationality, and modeling.[34] Klenke-Hamel's model indicates commitment is an outcome of job characteristics (as in Hackman and Oldham) and job-related stress, which in themselves are influenced by personal characteristics and organizational characteristics.[35] Wiener's normative model shows commitment is an outcome of generalized loyalty/duty and organizational identification, both of which are influenced by organizational socialization.[36]

Motivation

A difficulty in analyzing motivation in the context of organizational commitment is that motivation itself is an elusive concept. In the 1960s, Cattell and Cofer and Appley describe motivational research as chaotic, like blind men describing an elephant.[37] Views from the 1980s are similar.[38] The Hackman-Oldham perspective illustrates some of the difficulties: Problems of work motivation are related more to the job than to personality disposition.[39]

Such a position is seen to be fundamentally at odds with some of the basic motivational tenets; for example, Lewin's B = f (P, E), Getzels' B = f (R, P), and Cattell's "ergic tension" model;[40] and also some recent views, such as those of Wiener for whom constitutional and biological components are integral to the model.[41] Another difficulty with the Hackman-Oldham perspective is *responsibility*: Not all individuals seek autonomy on the job; some prefer *dependency*.[42] This is certainly contrary to the Watergate matter. But, in a more general work context, if superior-subordinate interaction is the single most important organizational variable contributing to stress on the job,[43] then the model of man proposed by Hackman-Oldham is one who must function at type I, type IIA value systems. This means that no one in the work place works according to the pace of others (contrary to the Hawthorne studies) or works for the pleasure of it.

Despite these negative observations, it is convenient to think of motivation in terms of arousal, or needs and choice, or intention (e.g., goal setting, expectancy, equity). This is the position of Mitchell and Rummel, a position they prefer because man has a choice with the inclusion of intention.[44] This basic dichotomy has long-standing philosophical correlates (e.g., Aristotle's vegetative, sentient, and rational principles) as well as contemporary philosophical correlates, specifically, Hodgkinson's. Choice is incorporated in type IIA and type IIB values; needs in type III values. The matter of intentionality has an implied component, the will, which is a component of type I values.

Freedom

Intentionality implies more than rational processing, which is seen as dominant in choice theories. Weiner incorporates volition in his model of attribution as a third causal dimension (in addition to stability and locus of control).[45] In other words, will. This is a radical departure from orthodox psychology, first enunciated by William James.[46] James' problem was that he could not reconcile philosophical and psychological perspectives of choice. Bieliauskas called for reconciliation in 1973;[47] Hodgkinson provides a cogent rapprochement. At issue is the will, which cannot be measured, and, consequently, logical positivists will discount it. Yet moral commitment (which implies will) is an acknowledged type of commitment.

Roles

There are numerous studies that relate roles to commitment. Kanter has commitment to social roles as one of three types of commitment.[48] Katz sees dependable role behavior as essential to organizational member behavior.[49] Connor and Becker view roles as part of the organizational process facilitating commitment.[50] Scholl sees role performance as a result of commitment.[51] Hodgkinson views the first phase of organizational commitment as commitment to roles through socialization. Schein sees pivotal and peripheral role behavior as integral to commitment.[52] Buchanan states that commitment to one's role in relation to the goals and values of the organization is one of three organizational commitment components.[53]

Empirical role analysis in an organizational context, which began in the 1950s, revealed how attitudes are shaped by roles,[54] how role conflict varies with the incompatibility of role expectations,[55] and how role conflict is resolved.[56] The seminal work of Kahn et al. appeared in the following decade and was subsequently incorporated in the work of Katz and Kahn.

The impact of role occupancy in the commitment process is evident. It begs the question, Can there be commitment to the organization without commitment to the role? At the very least, roles would seem to mediate individual commitment to organizations.

A PHENOMENOLOGICAL VIEW OF COMMITMENT

Researchable Question

The above material suggests the fundamental question: Is there a typology of organizational commitment that corresponds to Hodgkinson's value typology? It is acknowledged that there are moral and calculative types of commitment, which could be viewed as type I and type IIA, respectively. Milgram's work, specifically his agentic state,[57] could be viewed as consensual, type IIB commitment. Research relating to pleasure-based commitment (type III) is not readily available, even though some acknowledge the significance of emotions in the commitment process.[58]

Design

A number of factors influenced the design of the two studies reported here. Value and value systems are recognized as personal and subjective.[59] Substantive empirical data show a cultural effect in organizational commitment: traditional antecedent variables cannot explain commitment.[60] Because commitment is so personal,[61] some social scientists would view the phenomenological approach as the best methodology.[62] Primary data for both studies are derived from interviews.

The Two Studies

One study is based on interviews with fifty-four officers of the rank of major in the Canadian Forces. The second study is based on eight civilians, two from each of four organizations (a major church, a major bank, the British Columbia Legislature, and an amateur choral group). In the military study, ten officers were identified for interviews by their scores on the Organizational Commitment Questionnaire (OCG):[63] the five high scorers and the five low scorers. In the civilian study, interviewees were identified by gatekeepers[64] from their respective organizations as being highly committed. The Commitment Interview Schedule, developed by the author, was used for all interviewees in both studies.[65]

Military Study

Scores on the OCQ determined high or low group membership. Midpoint score on the OCQ is four: the five in the high group all had scores above six; the five in the low group all had scores below four.

From the perspective of type I value responses in interview data, it is virtually impossible to distinguish high-group members from low-group members. Typical of low-group responses to explain their sense of commitment: "I have a deep sense of duty and obligation because of my commission"; "It's a moral thing isn't it?" The difference between the high and low groups is very clear from the perspective of type IIA values (pragmatic values). Four of the five high-group members explained their sense of commitment in terms of type IIA values; none of the low-group members gave similar evidence. Typical high-group responses: "You have to have commitment so as never to bring discredit upon the service"; "The responsibility to your subordinates is critical"; "The combined efforts of all of us can motivate the younger ones"; "I have never lost that sense of responsibility in leading NCOs." No such responses came from low-group members. From the perspective of type IIB values (consensus), there were only two responses from all ten protocols that could be interpreted as type IIB, one from each group. However, from the perspective of type III values (emotional), the groups differ considerably. Typical responses from low-group members:

I meet the requirements of my commission. I have a commission as a naval officer. You can forget the rest of the CF [Canadian Forces].

My commitment was constant up to three years ago. At that time there was a problem regarding a posting. Another fellow got what I wanted because I think he squeaked louder.

About seven years ago my commitment was about 50% because I was looking for a job.

I feel self-conscious about wearing a green uniform downtown. The problem is this: I can't show the world what I am. [He is a naval officer.]

There were no statements of this nature from the high group.

Although the interview transcripts amount to twenty pages, it would appear that these samples convey the complexity of the commitment process. The members of the low group give clear evidence of disenchantment; the high group do not. The significance of role occupancy is clearly evident in the "self-conscious" officer. This same officer also stated this: "I have 100% commitment. I serve with love and no illusions. I'm a slave—but a loyal slave." During the interview with this officer, one could readily sense his emotional turmoil (about having to wear green) but also his undeniable affection for the navy. This sort of emotional involvement as a reaction to major organization change (integration of Canadian Forces) is similar to that reported by Hall, Schneider, and Nygren in their study of Roman Catholic priests and Vatican II. An obvious question: Why do some react this way? The intepretation can be seen from the type of value-based commitment involved. If type III values (emotions) dominate organization involvement—"I'm in because I like it"—then recourse to a higher type of value involvement is ineffective. Further substantiation for this is found in the civilian study.

The absence of substantive type IIB value (consensus) statements is understandable if one accepts the premise that officers of the rank of major are supposed to be leaders and that a leadership philosophy based on the principle of consensus is generally acknowledged to be quite ineffective; it contradicts initiative.

Although effective involvement in the military may be dependent upon Barnard's notion of communion,[66] the military itself is a pragmatic organization characterized by Weberian bureaucracy. Type IIA comments by members of the high group are consistent with this perspective. Absence of similar data from low-group members would suggest that they do not have the same perspective; they are committed, but from a different value-based perspective.

When both high- and low-commitment groups are compared in the context of value type responses, both groups gave strong evidence of type I values and no evidence of type IIB values; the high group gave strong evidence of type IIA values (whereas the low group did not); and the low group gave strong evidence of type III values (the high group did not). Furthermore, only the low group gave evidence of disenchantment with the military. At the same time, however, some low-group members can be said to be highly committed. These are not contradictory statements; they illustrate the complexity of commitment. It would seem that an understanding of the consequences of role occupancy is integral to commitment. It is not enough just to believe in or like the organization, or one's involvement in it. One must be prepared to want to do it (role enactment). A question which arises in this context is: "Does this hold true for all types of organizations?" This and other questions were investigated in the second study.

Civilian Study

Based on the previous study and literature, it was deemed necessary to clarify three important concepts: organization ideology, organization culture, and organization climate.[67] Organization ideology refers to the fundamental beliefs and value systems of the organization. It answers the question: What does the organization stand for? Organization culture refers to the norms of the organization that are guideposts for behaviors. Organization climate refers to the techniques used by organization members to effect the socialization process. Viewed this way, an ideology infuses a culture, giving it life as it were. Ideologies are manifested in cultures. And culture determines the organizational behavioral parameters—the do's and don't's—for membership. Climate is something specific, measurable, and manipulative (e.g., leadership style, personnel support systems, the perception that the organization looks after its members). This hierarchical order is isomorphic with Hodgkinson's value typology. Ideology is transrational, belief based. Culture supplies both logic-based and consensual-based justifications for behavior. Climate appeals to affective states. It is making an individual *feel* that he is important, that what he does is important, that he will be looked after.

The above concepts led to the formulation of four hypotheses: (1) The ideology of organizations is of four types: transrational, utilitarian, consensual, and hedonic; (2) organization ideology is a function of the purpose of the organization; (3) the commitment of individuals to organizations is of four types: transrational, utilitarian, consensual, and hedonic; and (4) the commitment of individuals to organizations is a congruent function of organization ideology.

Data to support these hypotheses were derived as follows: Eight experts in organizational behavior gave unanimous/majority evaluations of thirty-six organizations in the context of Hodgkinson's value typology. Gatekeepers from thirty of the thirty-six organizations generated statements of organization purpose, which were evaluated by a laymen sample of nurses, teachers, secretaries, and university students from the same perspective of expert jury; similar evaluations were achieved on twenty of the thirty organizations. The church, bank, legislature, and amateur choral group were evaluated similarly by expert and laymen samples as transrational, utilitarian, consensual, and hedonic, respectively. Gatekeepers from these organizations generated statements of organization ideology—by answering the question, "What does the organization stand for?"—and a list of at least five highly committed individuals (using the Mowday et al. interpretation). Two individuals from each organization agreed to in-depth interviews, using the Commitment Interview Schedule.[68] These protocols were subsequently evaluated by five judges (a psychiatrist, a psychologist, a social worker, an English professor, and an education specialist) in the context of Hodgkinson's value typology and achieved an overall hit rate of 65% with expert jury data.[69] Statements of organization ideology were evaluated by another sample of teachers, university students, and secretaries, similarly to the expert jury data.

The interview protocols did convey a typology of commitment which can be described as transrational, utilitarian, consensual, and hedonic. Faith in God was the dominant theme of the clergymen. Although there was strong evidence that they enjoyed their involvement (type III), their faith kept them there. The bankers' involvement was pragmatic (type IIA). The legislators' protocols gave evidence of faith in the political system (type I) and enjoyment (type III), but they also made it clear that without consensus in the House and "consenting to the will of the electorate" (Type IIB), they could not attain or maintain political power, which they stated to be "the name of the game." The choral group members were very clear that they were involved "for the pleasure of good choral music" (type III) and that their continued involvement was totally dependent upon that; should enjoyment disappear, they would leave.

IMPLICATIONS FOR ORGANIZATIONAL BEHAVIOR

Denhardt and Hodgkinson consider *praxis* integral to proper organizational behavior,[70] especially at the senior administrative level. *Praxis* is an Aristotelian term meaning practical wisdom; it is the combination of reason and values; it is purposeful human behavior, value based. *Praxis* embodies organizational ideology, culture, and climate from the perspective of person-as-organization-member and person-as-individual. What does this mean for the soldier? It means that, although he is ultimately responsible to himself for his own behavior (ethics), he is, at the same time, responsible for his expected role-related behavior. The extent to which he is committed to role enactment depends upon the nature of that value-based commitment.

Consider the account of Eli Geva, who as an Israeli brigade commander asked to be relieved of command rather than execute orders from higher command.[71] Based on these two accounts, Geva was—and probably still is—highly committed to the Israeli Army. Instead of granting his request to be relieved of command, the Israeli Army dismissed him. According to the accounts, Geva's request to be relieved of command was influenced by two factors: his belief that his men would experience a high casualty rate and that many elderly people and children would also become casualties. In his analysis of commitment, Werkmeister would explain Geva's commitment, and decision making, as a matter of values.[72]

It is suggested here that Geva's decision to ask to be relieved of command was based on a set of transrational values (type I). While it is true that calculative elements (type IIA), i.e., casualty rate and career implications, were involved in the decision-making process, his fundamental belief systems of man *qua* man were at the transrational level.

Geva's commitment to the Israeli Army transcends the rationality of the military as a Weberian bureaucratic organization.

His own values became the final arbiter. If Geva's commitment to the Israeli Army is viewed from the perspective of organization ideology (what the Israeli Army stands for), it can be safely stated that his commitment is strong. If viewed from the perspective of organization culture (standardized ways of thinking and acting in the Israeli Army), his commitment is conditional: conditional in the sense that the values associated with role expectations are not in conflict with his values. When conflict does arise, his type I values will dominate—and he will do what he did.

The balancing of one's personal values with those of the organization is not a simple feat. It is all too easy to say, "I do not believe in doing that, and therefore ask to be excused." Such an attitude harbors dereliction of responsibilities. Codes for ethical behavior have been developed from earliest times (e.g., Bhagavad-Gita) to the present (e.g., Gabriel's *To Serve with Honor*). But what these codes cannot do is tell an individual what he or she *must* do in any specific ethical dilemma. No code exists that could have told Eli Geva what to do. Nor will there ever be such a code. The explanation is straightforward: man, by his nature, has a free will. He alone must decide what to do. However, in the exercise of that free will, it is incumbent upon him to act with enlightened conscience. To retreat into one's inner values without due regard to the rational demands of office (role occupancy) is to risk legitimate role expectations. Such actions may be termed imprudent. On the other hand, to retreat into one's role expectations without due regard to one's inner values is to risk agentic type behavior.[73] The man of practical wisdom evaluates his own values in the context of role expectations, makes a decision, and acts. In so doing he will be both praised and damned.

COMMITMENT AND LEGITIMACY

The fundamental question of this whole chapter could be stated thus: "When an individual makes a commitment, to what extent is he obliged to fulfill it?" The answer lies in the nature of commitment and the meaning of legitimacy.

Commitment

The position taken in this chapter is that the commitment of individuals to organizations is essentially a conscious, value-based process. This commitment may be one of three types, or a combination of them: transrational (type I), which involves matters of belief, faith, and will; rational, which is either pragmatic and utilitarian (type IIA) or consensual (type IIB); or subrational (type III), which is emotional or pleasure based. Furthermore, there is a hierarchical order to these types. Finally, there is a positive relationship between commitment type and organization ideology (what the organization stands for).

Legitimacy

In the context of organizational behavior, legitimacy would seem to involve three fundamental concepts: organization rules, laws of the state, and universally accepted principles of human behavior.[74] Space does not permit a careful delineation of these concepts as they might apply to the soldier. Nevertheless it is important to make certain statements, amplification of which can be found in relevent texts.[75] First, matters of legitimacy are resolved ultimately on philosophical grounds. Second, there is a natural moral law. Natural signifies the essence of man *qua* man, in other words, the rational powers (intellect and will); moral signifies the free acts of man; and law signifies order. Third, certain universal laws of behavior are natural to man (moral law); these principles are innate to man *qua* man, not derived from reason. (This is the Thomistic-Kantian distinction, where Kant developed his categorical imperatives, much as an experimental psychologist posits hypothetical constructs.)[76] Fourth, the moral law is a human law, but it is not man-made. Fifth, man-made laws can generally be interpreted as determined from moral law (e.g., murder is against state law (*ius civile*) as consistent with moral law (*ius gentium*). Sixth, moral acts are particularistic, individualistic, voluntary, concrete acts. Moral law transcends state law. The obligations of moral law cannot be exhausted by legal treatment of rights and duties.[77] Seventh, there is a real and logical distinction between knowledge of ethics and acting ethically (prudence). These issues constitute the foundation of moral behavior for the person-as-individual.

For the person-as-organization-member there are positive laws, instituted by man, determined to be for the good of the community. The question as to whether these are "laws" is discussed by Adler,[78] who prefers "rules" because of the nature of obligation involved: matters of natural law (*ius naturalae*) are principles; matters of moral law (*ius gentium*) are precepts; and matters of state law (*ius civile*) are rules. State laws are mutable, man-made, imperfect, and community specific (e.g., one drives to the right in North America, to the left in England). State laws are specific *means* to man's end in the context of natural law. Moral law (precepts) and natural law (principles) are immutable, implanted in man, and universal. Moral law is a *conclusion* from natural law; state law is *determined* from moral law; moral law is the universal means to natural law. Obligation to state law is extrinsic; obligation to moral law is intrinsic. For the person-as-organization-member he is obliged to obey organization rules but only on the condition that these rules have been determined from moral law and have the quality of justice. (It was this proviso which set some German generals against Adolf Hitler.)[79]

The conflict between the obligations of the person-as-individual and the obligations of the person-as-organization-member was dealt at length by Barnard,[80] but the difficulty with his interpretation of moral behavior (moral code) is that he involves the sentient principle of life (Aristotelian) in moral decision making, which is fundamentally at odds with the Thomistic view. A consequence of this is that the real and logical distinction between the obligations inherent in moral precepts and organization rules becomes blurred, reducing moral precepts to matters of man-made rules. Two major works which require special consideration in this issue are Cooper's *The Responsible Administrator*[81] and Gabriel's *To Serve with Honor*.

Cooper emphasizes the relationship between ethics and values. The leader is ethical to the extent that he or she performs a value audit in the context of decision making, being fully conscious of the end that is being served by his or her values. This is the very point inherent in the three commitment types. As with Hodgkinson, Cooper's concern is that organizational conflict is essentially a conflict of values (as McMurray[82] stated so clearly)—that some individuals may be expressing immutable moral codes (type I values) while others are expressing emotive values (type III values). Cooper is very clear that the ethical leader rank orders his or her value systems. Furthermore, Cooper is equally clear about the consequences of role occupancy: It is the responsibility of the leader to evaluate the impact of role occupancy (and all that that entails) upon his or her value system. This is the fulcrum for balancing obligations to self as person-as-individual and obligations to others as person-as-organization member.

Much of Gabriel's Soldier's Code of Ethics[83] is transorganizational, a restatement of moral precepts. But there are problems. Gabriel would have us all responsible for everyone's actions, in an organizational context. However, he also advocates that each member be responsible for his or her own behavior. This latter statement is consistent with the generally held view of moral philosophy. But his former statement is difficult to comprehend because it contradicts not only his statement of ethical responsibility, but also the very nature of the military as a Weberian bureaucracy—surely the private is not responsible for the captain's actions? Who was responsible for what Eli Geva did? Gabriel's military ethics would seem to make more sense if viewed as a set of organization rules, *ius organizatio* perhaps, because what he advocates is logically impossible: the plurality of that which is fundamentally, essentially individualistic, particularistic—and subjective. The key concept is values. He is imposing a set of values which precludes freedom of the will. He comes dangerously close to falling into logical positivism, where "is" determines "ought." "Here is the code. You have no choice." His view of man *qua* man has to be that he espouse solely type I values, which ontologically puts him in with the angels (and even they had problems).

The fundamental Thomistic view of man's obligation to organization rules is that he is obliged to obey with the proviso that they are determined from moral law and have the quality of justice. The reason is straightforward: the good of the community takes precedence over the good of the individual. All members of an organization are morally obliged to obey the rules of their organization, but an offense against an organization rule is not a direct offense against moral law. No court or tribunal can pass judgment on any moral act; judgment can be passed only on offenses against man-made laws and thereby *infer* degrees of moral behavior.

Commitment and Legitimacy in the Military

An attempt will be made to answer the question posed earlier: "When an individual makes a commitment, to what extent is he obliged to fulfill it?" First, commitment resides solely within the soldier, as person-as-individual. It is something he gives to the military and, as noted previously, his commitment is essentially a conscious, value-based process (hence, personal and subjective) and is fundamentally one of three types, or a combination of the three. Second, legitimacy resides solely in the soldier's role, as person-as-organization-member. Role determines his legitimacy to act, commensurate with organization rules. Third, obligation for the soldier to act resides within his own being (person-as-individual) *and* within the role he occupies (person-as-organization-member). Fourth, regardless of the nature of his commitment, the soldier is morally obliged to obey the rules of his military organization. He is also morally obliged to disobey any rules or orders that he *believes* to be contrary to precepts of moral law. However, it must be clearly understood that this kind of action necessitates informed conscience. Before he disobeys, hs is morally obliged to evaluate his own values and beliefs with those of the military.

The matter of informed conscience is the fulcrum that balances instrinsic and extrinsic obligations. Conscience is a practical judgment based on knowledge (*cum scientia*). When matters of doubt arise, the soldier is required, morally, to ascertain as much knowledge as possible, prior to making his judgment. (It is at this point that organization gatekeepers exert their influence.) In the final analysis, the soldier must make a decision, one which is value based, and live with the consequences.

Values determine the extent to which an individual is obliged to fulfill his commitment. This is always a self-imposed obligation. This does not mean that the soldier necessarily enjoys what he has to do or even agrees with what must be done. What is meant here is that it is the soldier's value system that determines his commitment and the extent to which he will fulfill that commitment.

NOTES

1. C. Hodgkinson, *Towards a Philosophy of Administration* (Oxford: Basil Blackwell, 1978); C. Hodgkinson, *The Philosophy of Leadership* (Oxford: Basil Blackwell, 1983); and D. Lang, "Values and Commitment: An Empirical Verification of Hodgkinson's Value Paradigm as Applied to the Commitment of Individuals to Organizations," Ph.D. diss., University of Victoria, Victoria, B.C., Canada, 1986.

2. D. Katz and R. Kahn, *The Social Psychology of Organizations*, 2nd ed. (Toronto: John Wiley & Sons, 1978).

3. T. Girdon, *Current Military Values* (Newport, R.I.: U.S. Naval War College, Center for Advanced Research, June 1980).

4. W. Oates, *Aristotle and the Problem of Value* (Princeton, N.J.: Princeton University Press, 1963).

5. C. Barnard, *The Functions of the Executive* (Cambridge, Mass.: Harvard University Press, 1938).

6. W. French, *The Personnel Management Process*, 4th ed. (Boston: Houghton Mifflin Company, 1978), and F. Luthans, *Organizational Behavior*, 3rd ed. (Toronto: McGraw-Hill, 1981).

7. R. McMurray, "Conflicts in Human Values," *Harvard Business Review*, May-June 1963, pp. 130–45.

8. T. Cooper, "Ethics, Values and Systems," *Journal of Systems Management*, September 1979, pp. 6–12.

9. In 1967, R.B. Cattell, *The Scientific Analysis of Personality* (New York: Penguin Books, 1967), p. 264, held that value measurement is not yet possible. P. Connor and B. Becker, "Values and the Organization: Suggestions for Research," *Academy of Management Journal* 18 (1975), p. 71, are deliberately vague on the operational use of the concept of value; they cite M. Rokeach, *The Nature of Human Values* (London: The Free Press, 1973), p. 559, who maintains that it is not yet conceptually meaningful or technicologically feasible to measure values.

10. H. Simon, *Administrative Behavior*, 2nd ed. (New York: Free Press, 1957); B.F. Skinner, *Beyond Freedom and Dignity* (New York: Bantam/Vintage Books, 1971); and J. Fodor, "The Mind-Body Problem," *Scientific American* 244 (1981), pp. 114–23.

11. C. Kluckhohn, "Values and Value-Orientations in the Theory of

Action: An Exploration in Definition and Classification," in *Toward a General Theory of Action*, ed. T. Parsons and E. Shils (Cambridge, Mass.: Harvard University Press, 1952), pp. 388–433; Rokeach, *The Nature of Human Values*; V. Vroom, *Work and Motivation* (Toronto: John Wiley & Sons, Inc., 1964); and E. Locke, "Work Motivation Theories," in *International Review of Industrial and Organizational Psychology 1986*, ed. C.L. Cooper and I.T. Robertson (Toronto: Wiley, 1986).

12. M. Weber, *The Theory of Social and Economic Organization*, trans. A.M. Henderson and T. Parsons (London: The Free Press of Glencoe, 1947).

13. J. Burns, *Leadership* (New York: Harper & Row, 1978); T. Jacobs, *Leadership and Exchange in Formal Organizations* (Alexandria, Va.: Human Resources Research Organization, 1971); and E. Schein, *Organizational Psychology*, 2nd ed. (Englewood Cliffs, N.J.: Prentice-Hall Inc., 1970).

14. C. Moskos, "From Institution to Occupation," *Armed Forces and Society* 4 (1977), pp. 41–50, and R. Mowday, L. Porter, and R. Steers, *Employee-Organization Linkages: The Psychology of Commitment, Absenteeism, and Turnover* (Toronto: Academic Press, 1982).

15. J. Getzels and E. Guba, "Role, Role Conflict, and Effectiveness: An Empirical Study," *American Sociological Review* 19 (1954), pp. 164–75.

16. C. Cotton, *Military Attitudes and Values of the Army in Canada*, Report No. 79–5 (Toronto: Canadian Forces Personnel Applied Research Unit, December 1979), and R. Gabriel, *To Serve with Honor: A Treatise on Military Ethics and the Way of the Soldier* (Westport, Conn: Greenwood Press, 1982).

17. A. Etzioni, *A Comparative Analysis of Complex Organizations* (New York: Free Press, 1961); R.M. Kanter, "Commitment and Social Organization: A Study of Commitment Mechanisms in Utopian Communities," *American Sociological Review* 33 (1968), pp. 499–517; and D. Hall and B. Schneider, *Organizational Climates and Careers* (New York: Seminar Press, 1973).

18. Mowday, Porter, and Steers, *Employee-Organization Linkages*.

19. B. Staw and G. Salancik, *New Directions in Organizational Behavior* (Chicago: St. Clair Press, 1977).

20. J. Alutto, L. Hrebiniak, and R. Alonso, "On Operationalizing the Concept of Commitment," *Social Forces* 51 (1973), pp. 448–54; L. Hrebiniak and J. Alutto, "Personal and Role-Related Factors in the Development of Organizational Commitment," *Administrative Science Quarterly* 17 (1972), pp. 552–72; and R. Mowday, R. Steers, and L. Porter, "The Measurement of Organizational Commitment," *Journal of Vocational Behavior* 13 (1979), pp. 224–47.

21. R. Steers, "Antecedents and Outcomes of Organizational Commitment," *Administrative Science Quarterly* 22 (1977), pp. 46–56.

22. Mowday, Porter, and Steers, *Employee-Organization Linkages*.

23. H. Angle and J. Perry, "An Empirical Assessment of Organizational Commitment and Organizational Effectiveness," *Administrative Science Quarterly* 26 (1981), pp. 1–14; E. Benjamin, "Participation and the Attitude of Organizational Commitment: A Study of Quality Circles," *Dissertation Abstracts International* 43, 2062–B (University Microfilms No. 8301904, 1982); D. Hall, B. Schneider, and H. Nygren, "Personal Factors in Organizational Identification," *Administrative Science Quarterly* 15 (1970), pp. 176–90; and A. Kidron, "Work Values and Organizational Commitment," *Academy of Management Journal* 21 (1978), pp. 239–47.

24. Etzioni, *Comparative Analysis of Complex Organizations*.

25. W. Werkmeister, *Man and His Values* (Lincoln: University of Nebraska Press, 1967).

26. Benjamin, "Participation."

27. J. Bowles, "An Investigation of Organizational Commitment, Facet Satisfaction, and Intent to Remain among Faculty of Selected Tennessee Institutions of Higher Education." *Dissertation Abstracts International* 44, 922–A (University Microfilms No. 8319312, 1983); R. Laud, "Organizational Commitment and Value Placed on Job Autonomy as a Function of Work Orientation, Age, Group, and Professional Job Group," *Dissertation Abstracts International* 43, 3521–A (University Microfilm No. 8307599, 1982); and J. Stengel, "Faculty Commitment to Administratively Defined Organizational Goal Priorities," *Dissertation Abstracts International* 44, 949–A (University Microfilms No. 8315826, 1983).

28. A. Eblen, "Communication, Gender, Leadership and Commitment in the Organization," *Dissertation Abstracts International* 44, 2291–A (University Microfilms No. 8325263, 1983), and T. Sullivan, "Organizational Commitment, Job Satisfaction, and Leadership Behaviors within Residential Facilities for the Mentally Retarded," *Dissertation Abstracts International* 43, 3064–B (University Microfilms No. 8303641, 1982).

29. M. Feltham, "A Study of Role Stress Conflict, Role Stress Ambiguity, Participation in Decision Making, and Social Support in Relation to Job Satisfaction and to Organizational Commitment among Professional Nurses," *Dissertation Abstracts International* 44, 2706–B (University Microfilms No. 8329820, 1983), and A. Reichers, "Conflict and Organizational Commitment," *Dissertation Abstracts International* 44, 809–A (University Microfilms No. 8315498, 1983).

30. M. Stahl, C. McNichols, and T. Manley, "An Empirical Examination of the Moskos Institution-Occupation Model," *Armed Forces and Society* 6 (1980), pp. 257–69.

31. Moskos' position is that the U.S. military is becoming civilianized and, consequently, "occupational." He sees this as dysfunctional. Janowitz contends, however, that there is no cause for alarm. M. Janowitz, "From Institutional to Occupational," *Armed Forces and Society* 4 (1977), pp. 51–54.

32. Y. Wiener, in "Commitment in Organizations: A Normative View," *Academy of Management Review* 7 (1982), pp. 418–28, states that models should meet three criteria: definitional precision, theoretical integration with other relevant constructs, and predictive power. K. Klenke-Hamel, in "Causal Modeling of Organizational Commitment," *Dissertation Abstracts International* 43, 3764–B (University Microfilms No. 8306288, 1982), p. 17, sees models as useful tools for examining multiple relationships within a set of variables.

33. J. Stevens, J. Beyer, and H. Trice, "Assessing Personal, Role, and Organizational Predictors of Managerial Commitment," *Academy of Management Journal* 21 (1978), pp. 380–96, and R. Kahn, D. Wolfe, R. Quinn, J. Snoek, and R. Rosenthal, *Organizational Stress: Studies in Role Conflict and Ambiguity* (New York: Wiley, 1964).

34. B. Staw, "The Escalation of Commitment to a Course of Action," *Academy of Management Review* 6 (1981), pp. 577–87.

35. Klenke-Hamel, "Causal Model."

36. Wiener, "Commitment in Organizations," pp. 418–28.

37. Cattell, *Scientific Analysis of Personality*, and C. Cofer and M. Appley, *Motivation: Theory and Research* (New York: Wiley, 1964).

38. N. Brody, "Social Motivation," *Annual Review of Psychology* 31 (1981), pp. 143–68: J. Reykowski, "Social Motivation," *Annual Review of Psychology* 33 (1982), pp. 123–54; and F. Landy, *Adaptive Motivation Theory*, Report No. NR 170–926 (U.S. Office of Naval Research, Arlington, Va., February 1982).

39. J. Hackman and G. Oldham, *Work Redesign* (Reading, Mass.: Addison-Wesley, 1980).

40. K. Lewin, *A Dynamic Theory of Personality* (New York: McGraw-Hill, 1935); J. Getzels, "A Social Psychology of Education," in *Handbook of Social Psychology*, ed. G. Lindzey and E. Aronson, 2nd ed., vol. 5 (Reading, Mass.: Addison-Wesley, 1969), pp. 459–537; and Cattell, *Scientific Analysis of Personality*.

41. Wiener, "Commitment in Organizations."

42. Hackman and Oldham, *Work Redesign*.

43. Kahn et al., *Organizational Stress*, and F. Fieldler, "Are Leaders

an Intelligent Form of Life? The Role of Cognitive Processes in Leadership Performance," Tech. Rep. No. 81–1 (Seattle: University of Washington, Center for Organizational Research, 1982).

44. T. Mitchell, "Motivation: New Directions for Theory, Research, and Practice," *Academy of Management Review* 7 (1982), pp. 80–88, and R. Rummel, *Understanding Conflict and War*, Vol. 1 (Toronto: Wiley, 1975).

45. B. Weiner, *Cognitive Views of Motivation* (New York: Academic Press, Inc., 1974).

46. W. James, *The Principles of Psychology*, Vol. 2 (New York: Dover Publications, Inc., 1890).

47. V. Bieliauskas, "Motivation and the Will," in *Alfred Adler: His Influence on Psychology Today*, ed. H. Mosak (Park Ridge, N.J.: Noyes Publications, 1973).

48. Kanter, "Commitment and Social Organization."

49. D. Katz, "The Motivational Basis of Organizational Behavior," *Behavioral Science* 9 (1964), pp. 131–46.

50. Connor and Becker, "Values and the Organization," pp. 550–61.

51. R. Scholl, "Differentiating Organizational Commitment from Expectancy as a Motivating Force," *Academy of Management Review* 6 (1981), pp. 589–99.

52. Schein, *Organizational Psychology*.

53. B. Buchanan, "Building Organizational Commitment: The Socialization of Managers in Work Organizations," *Administrative Science Quarterly* 19 (1974), pp. 533–46.

54. S. Lieberman, "The Effects of Changes on the Attitudes of Role Occupants," *Human Relations* 9 (1956), pp. 385–402.

55. N. Gross, W. Mason, and R. McEachern, *Explorations in Role Analysis: Studies of the School Superintendency Role* (New York: Wiley, 1958).

56. Getzels and Guba, "Role, Role Conflicts, and Effectiveness."

57. S. Milgram, *Obedience to Authority: An Experimental View* (New York: Harper & Row, 1974).

58. Hall and Schneider, *Organizational Climates*, p. 141, write: "The attitude about the organization developed by the individual in response to the fulfillment of the psychological contract can be termed his organizational commitment or identification defined as the degree of emotional attraction he feels for the organization." This is type III commitment.

59. Hodgkinson, *Towards a Philosophy of Administration*, *The Philosophy of Leadership*, and Kluckhohn, "Values and Value-Orientation."

60. The best example of this is the longitudinal study by R. Marsh

and H. Mannari, "Organizational Commitment and Turnover: A Prediction Study," *Administrative Science Quarterly* 22 (1977), pp. 57–75.

61. At a symposium dealing with organizational commitment, Professor Porter commented that, although an organization has every right to expect obedience from its members, it can only hope for commitment. D. Lang, "Commitment in the Military Profession," paper presented at a symposium conducted at Royal Roads Military College, Victoria, B.C., Canada, December 1983.

62. T.B. Greenfield, "Reflections on Organizational Theory and the Truths of Irreconcilable Realities," *Educational Administration Quarterly* 14 (1978), pp. 1–23; J. Van Maanen, "Reclaiming Qualitative Methods for Organizational Research: A Preface," *Administrative Science Quarterly* 24 (1979), pp. 520–26; F. Luthans and T. Davis, "An Idiographic Approach to Organizational Behavior Research: The Use of Single Case Experimental Designs and Direct Measures," *Academy of Management Review* 7 (1982), pp. 380–91; and R. Evered and M. Louis, "Alternative Perspectives in the Organizational Sciences: 'Inquiry from the inside' and 'Inquiry from the outside,' " *Academy of Management Review* 6 (1981), pp. 385–95.

63. High-commitment group scores: 6.8, 6.8, 6.7, 6.5, and 6.4. Low-commitment group scores: 3.1, 3.5, 3.5, 3.5, and 3.9 D. Lang, "The Nature of Organizational Commitment," Master's thesis, University of Victoria, Victoria, B.C., Canada, 1982.

64. Gatekeepers are those senior organization officials who may be said to be responsible for developing, implementing, and maintaining the organization's ideology, culture (norms for behavior), and climate (socialization techniques). This is consistent with Lewin's earlier views: "[Gatekeepers'] decision depends partly on their ideology, that is, the system of values and beliefs which determines what they consider to be 'good' or 'bad,' partly on the way they perceive the particular situation" (p. 198). K. Lewin, "Group Decision and Social Change," in *Readings in Social Psychology*, ed. E. MacCahy, T. Newcombe, and E. Hartley (Toronto: Holt, Rinehart and Winston, 1958), pp. 197–211.

65. The Commitment Interview Schedule was based on the work by Smith, Bruner, and White. Nine sets of questions deal with joining the organization, importance, affect, investment/expectations, meaning, goals, beliefs about man, responsibility, and leaving the organization. M. Smith, J. Bruner, and R. White, *Opinions and Personality* (New York: Wiley, 1964).

66. Barnard, *Functions of the Executive*.

67. There is a great deal of confusion as to what these terms mean. S. Barley, G. Mayer, and D. Gash, "Cultures of Culture: Academics,

Practioners and the Pragmatics of Normative Control," *Administrative Science Quarterly* 33 (1888), pp. 24–60; A.M. Pettigrew, "On Studying Organizational Cultures," in *Qualitative Methodology*, ed. J. Van Maanen (Beverly Hills, Calif.: Sage, 1983); R. Weiss and L. Miller, "The Concept of Ideology in Organizational Analysis: The Sociology of Knowledge or the Social Psychology of Beliefs," *Academy of Management Review* 12, no. 1 (1987), pp. 104–16; and Y. Wiener, "Forms of Value Systems: A Focus on Organizational Effectiveness and Cultural Change and Maintenance," *Academy of Management Review* 13, no. 4 (1988), pp. 534–45.

68. Smith, Bruner, and White, *Opinions and Personality*.

69. The percentage was determined as follows: A value of 1 was assigned if a judge rank ordered the predicted outcome first; a value of 0.5 was assigned if the predicted outcome was ranked second; and a value of 0 was assigned if the predicted outcome was ranked third or fourth. (The four possible outcomes are the value types I; IIA; IIB; III). Five judges rated eight protocols. The judges' hit rate, by organization, was as follows: priests, 85 percent; bankers, 85 percent; legislators, 35 percent; and choir members, 55 percent.

70. R. Denhardt, *In the Shadow of Organization* (Lawrence, Kansas: Regents Press, 1981).

71. D. Gavnon, "Clash of Cymbals," *The Jerusalem Post Magazine* (June 10, 1983), p. 10.

72. Werkmeister, *Man and His Values*.

73. Milgram, *Obedience to Authority*.

74. Hodgkinson, *Towards a Philosophy*; Hodgkinson, *The Philosophy of Leadership*; Lang, *Values and Commitment*; and Gabriel, *To Serve with Honor*.

75. The two primary sources are V. Bourke, *Ethics: A Textbook in Moral Philosophy* (New York: Macmillan Company, 1953), and M. Adler, "A Question about Law," in *Essays in Thomism*, ed. R.E. Brennan (New York: Freeport, 1942), pp. 207–37. Both references give the Thomistic view of moral behavior. Adler gives a succinct metaphysical analysis of natural law (*ius naturalae*), moral law (*ius gentium*), and state law (*ius civile*), as well as positive law versus human law. Bourke gives a comprehensive analysis of the subject. The U.S. Army War College, Carlisle Barracks, has compiled a bibliography of 284 references (AD–A155009, March 1985).

76. Kant's categorical imperatives lead logically to the philosophy of utilitarianism. It is the supremacy of intellectual endowment as measured by Wechsler scales. It obviates the speculative intelligence of those who do not dwell on philosophical issues but none the less, know what is "right" and what is "wrong."

77. In *Ethics*, Bourke makes the distinction between moral obligations and duties of an extrinsic nature. Such duties are binding because of external force. There is a tendency to reduce ethics to matters of justice (pp. 180–82). In "A Question about Law," Adler cites the influence of logical positivism as the root cause for this tendency.

78. Adler, "A Question about Law."

79. J.W. Wheeler-Bennett, *The Nemesis of Power* (London: Macmillan & Co. Ltd., 1954). Hitler demanded personal and binding loyalty ("blind and unreasoning obedience") from his generals to himself instead of to the Republic: "the undertaking of this obligation had at the time caused grave searching of heart. But by the constant process of self-examination they arrived at the conclusion . . . that there were certain fealties to Germany, and even to humanity, which transcended any oath of loyalty exacted by monarch or Fuhrer. 'No Caesar and no King, no Dictator and no terror, can force me not to give to God the things which are God's,' wrote one of them" (p. 395). Wheeler-Bennett cites seven generals who remained steadfast to this division of loyalties. Their commitment could be described as type I. See p. 327 for the rise of the "careerist officer," who represents type IIA, calculative commitment.

80. Barnard, *Functions of the Executive*.

81. T. Cooper, *The Responsible Administrator: An Approach to Ethics for the Administrative Role* (Port Washington, N.Y.: National University Publications, 1982).

82. McMurray, "Conflicts in Human Values."

83. Gabriel, *To Serve with Honor*, pp. 140–47.

4

Commitment in Military Systems

Charles A. Cotton

The most important task in defense is the one most likely to be over-looked since it lies in the realm of character and values rather than in quantities that can be represented on charts. Before anything else, we must recognize that a functioning military requires bonds of trust, sacrifice, and respect within its ranks, and similar bonds of support and respect between an army and the nation it represents.

James Fallows[1]

The issue of commitment to military institutions, especially in the Canadian context, has interested and plagued this writer for more than a decade of graduate study, applied personnel research, and teaching in a Canadian military college. It began with a Master's thesis, entitled "Social Change and the Military: The Stabilization of Commitment," in the early 1970s which attempted to analyze how a phalanx of other analysts were engaged in similar conceptual work at that time. Societal and organizational trends in liberal democracies were eroding the traditional forms of involvement and commitment in military systems. To use Etzioni's typological distinctions, I was concerned with describing the shift from moral involvement to calculative involvement, a dynamic implicit in Moskos' conceptualization of trends in modern military organization.[2]

In my case, what in retrospect seems an exercise in creative macrosociology by assertion, led inexorably to the complex world of applied personnel research, dealing with such topics as recruitment, attrition, military value systems, and performance evaluation. Again and again, though, the concept of commitment provided a thread running through the technical research reports. At times, it was explicit, as in the case of a longitudinal study of over 5,000 graduates of Canadian military training schools, which examined the relationships among job satisfaction, organizational commitment as measured by the Organizational Commitment Questionnaire (OCQ) developed by Porter, and tenure in a military setting.[3] On other occasions, however, the concept of commitment was implicit, informing the research and providing a sort of hidden agenda, because the tautology is always there when one researches recruitment and turnover in organizational settings: problems indicate a relative lack of commitment among members. Setting aside the difficulties of operationalization and definition of the term, commitment is the sine qua non of effectiveness in volunteer military systems. Napoleon knew it, and I would venture to say that most soldiers still know it. The very best soldiers are concerned about it, although the magic formula remains as elusive today as it was two, or ten, centuries ago.

From the energetic world of bureaucratic research, this writer moved to a military college setting in which the primary goal was the developmental socialization of a highly committed future elite for the officer corps. A different world to be sure, but perhaps more challenging since one could not remain aloof in an observer capacity, but rather had to play an active role in the organization as process. Throughout my tenure, I have been struck by the fact that the majority of young cadets *are* organizationally committed, but in an instrumental way. In other words, most are *calculatively* involved; only a minority are *morally* involved, to return to Etzioni's terminology. On the other hand, the minority who have moral involvement, typically those in the traditional combat officer roles, seem frustrated with the attitudes of their peers and with the way in which they perceive the military to be developing through time. Frustration rises with the level of commitment, a proposition which was borne out in research into the structure of value orientations among serving Army personnel in the Canadian Forces.[4] This research, which involved an operationalization of Charles Moskos' conceptual model of occupational-institutional orientations to military service, pointed up the fact that the minority of highly committed, institutionally oriented combat officers were estranged from many force developments and serving members. These individuals, termed the "beleaguered warriors," were frustrated because they perceive a gap between what the military is and what it ought to be, and between how members define military service and how they ought to define it. The paraphrased comment of one experienced infantry officer—serving at the time in the Canadian Airborne Regiment—exemplified this paradox of high involvement (commitment) and high alienation: "I feel that most service members have forgotten that our primary role is to prepare for war. I find it increasingly difficult to relate to administrative heavy support personnel in the Canadian Forces. These civil servants in uniform need to get out of their offices, see what we are doing, and support us." His definition of the situation is widely shared by serving members who have what Moskos would term an "institutional" orientation toward military life and which I termed "vocational."

Thus both my everyday life in uniform and my research in the military have driven home to me time and time again the need for a phenomenological approach to the consideration of commitment in military systems—one which centers on organizational context and processes, as opposed to a static view of the organization as objective reality. The organization, in this case the military, is socially constructed, and it is different things to different participants. The view proposed here is developed and presented very clearly by Cummings.[5] He argues, very convincingly, that social scientists must focus on contexts and processes if they are to be able "to speak to issues of strategy, effectiveness, and survival at the organizational level and with meaning to the movers of organizations."[6]

It is my contention that the phenomenon of commitment is a central issue for the "movers" of military organizations and that it is fundamentally linked to institutional effectiveness and survival. It is necessary to move beyond the narrow, technical, and positivist approach to discussing and studying the matter, and to embed the discussion in the context and process of evolutionary change in military systems as social organizations with unique goals and requisites. In essence, this implies that the discussion must be "myth-centered," to use Cummings' terminology,[7] and to establish linkages with the myths and central cultural stories of senior leadership in the military. Without this, one confronts technical triviality and irrelevance, for the research and scholarly expositions will not make sense to the members of the tribe. In the end, in their essence, military systems are tribal and corporate, rather than instrumental and bureaucratic.

These introductory comments have been intended to set the stage for the reflections on commitment in military systems that follow. The thread that runs through those reflections is simple: commitment of members is a central problematic in military institutions, especially in a volunteer military of an advanced liberal democracy; military professionals must be concerned about the levels and types of commitment (although not necessarily study them through systematic research); and, we must analyze commitment in the context of unique operational requirements of military systems and the process of institutional change. In short, we need it, we need to be concerned about it, and we must be rather careful about how we talk about it. This last point is crucial; if we use the wrong rhetoric, we deny our own myths and become, as it were, part of the problem.

It seems appropriate to organize these various reflections around a set of linked assertions, or propositions, about commitment in military systems. Commitment here is used in its attitudinal rather than behavioral sense, along the lines suggested by Steers, Mowday, and Porter.[8] In conceptualizing organizational commitment, they refer to "the relative strength of an individual's identification with and involvement in a particular organization." At this point, it would be inappropriate to specify the organization, that is, the military, as the referent or focus of commitment, and I will initially refer to commitment as the relative strength of an individual's or individuals', identification with and involvement in a particular phenomenon. Thus people can be committed to a wide range of things, from groups to organizations, to ideologies, to families, and so on. We can speak of them being committed in a military context to their regiments, their traditions, their leaders, their country, their buddies, and so on. The variety of referents for commitment makes it an ambiguous and elusive concept.

While it would be easier, in this chapter, to adopt a tighter, narrower definition for commitment, it would not be especially relevant. Soldiers can be committed to many things, and their commitments are often in conflict. An a priori attempt to specify the referent narrowly lessens the potential for understanding context and process in military settings, and it increases the probability that we will miss the subtleties, complexities, and paradoxes of commitment. (This is not to imply that we do not encounter these even when we tightly conceptualize commitment to an organization, as pointed out by Steers, Mowday, and Porter.) However, since the concern here is with reflections, it is possible and advantageous to pursue a looser rather than a tighter conceptual line of thought. With this in mind, the following are offered:

Commitment is a fundamentally important institutional concern in the military, and leaders must be sensitive to that concern.

Although the concept of organizational commitment is of use in the descriptive and prescriptive analysis of military policies, it has limitations because of the unique nature of military goals.

It is dangerous and threatening to analyze commitment because the enemy may be ourselves.

These, of course, are not intended as propositions or hypotheses in the strict sense of social scientific enquiry; they are reflections only.

COMMITMENT IS A FUNDAMENTALLY IMPORTANT INSTITUTIONAL CONCERN IN THE MILITARY

Literally thousands of articles exist in military writing that deal with the issue of commitment and its linked concepts of morale, cohesion, esprit, combat motivation, and the ephemeral "will to fight." A lesser number, but still significant, can be found in the psychological and sociological literature on military institutions.[9] Commitment is one of the intangibles of military effectiveness referred to in the beginning quote in this chapter from James Fallows, and its centrality to the operational effectiveness of armed forces as systems of controlled violence is highlighted in Levy's very general treatment of them: "Military specialists for centuries have been aware of the fact that no equipment and no numbers give the members of any armed force organization superiority over others if they lack the will to fight."[10]

Minimally, leaders must be committed, in an attitudinal sense, as well as a minority of followers. The classic study by Shils and Janowitz on the performance of the German Army in the last years of World War II underscored the importance of soldierly commitment among leaders and a minority of ideologically committed soldiers.[11] To put this into a statistical frame of reference, it is not the average levels of commitment—however they are measured—among military participants which are important, but rather the distribution of commitment levels. A minority with high commitment will carry the others in a particular unit. It is necessary to go beyond the individual as the unit of analysis when discussing the role of commitment in military systems. There is a tendency to focus on the individual, especially in applied personnel research, to the detriment of analysis of collective and unit characteristics and behavior. Yet military operations are fundamentally collective, group modes of human action. For better or worse, the individual, either in the abstract or the concrete, is of secondary significance in military affairs, and, apart from great leaders or heroic individual actions, the culture of the military and its corporate philosophy are fundamentally group oriented. As Downey puts the point: "An armed force is a body of men organized to achieve its ends irresistibly by coordinated action. Cohesion is therefore the essence of its being."[12] And, to follow on the quote from Downey, I would argue that commitment is the essence of cohesion. Both are desired and scarce commodities in military systems.

The line of discussion being pursued here is quite obviously based on the premises that (1) military institutions are unique, (2) operational effectiveness is the first priority criterion in their analysis, and (3) the requirement for commitment among members is pronounced and organizationally more dramatic than in civilian organizations. Commitment to the point of death, what Hackett terms the unlimited liability clause of military members,[13] remains a distinguishing feature of the military. This of course is a central thread in the work of Morris Janowitz who has written of the limits to "civilianization" as long as the notion of "combat—preparation for battle and actual battle—remains a central military value."[14] In short, the military's requirement for commitment is derived from, and is conceptually and phenomenologically centered on, the battlefield. To use other frames of reference is to miss the institutional point entirely.

This is not to suggest, however, that other frames of reference are not useful in a limited context. Many models and metaphors are relevant to the analysis of personnel issues and dynamics in military systems, including the concept of organizational commitment referred to earlier in this chapter, but they must be used in the context of the raison d'être of the military. If linkages are not made to the central concerns of the military, and not made in terms that are meaningful to its leaders, some very sound research and analysis will be perceived as irrelevant at best, and dangerous at worst.

We may take the requirement for commitment in military systems as self-evident, and not belabor the point here, or burden ourselves with an exegesis of views to that effect. There remains, though, a set of rather thorny conceptual issues related to that truth, particularly in regard to the types and levels of commitment required and the "proper" foci of them. We in the military are not always clearheaded regarding these conceptual issues, and this is an area for serious and systematic investigation. Take, for example, the issue of "regimental commitment"—an attachment and value identification with one's regiment (or ship or squadron)—a valued military characteristic. How does this type and locus of commitment relate to a more global organizational commitment to, in Canada's case, the unified military bureaucracy? My own research has shown, for example, that support for regimental institutions and organizational commitment to the Canadian Forces are positively related. The simple correlation between measures of the two concepts is .22 among a sample of 1,667 serving Army personnel, a finding which is significant at the .001 level.[15] However, this relationship, as we shall see below, is lower than the relationships between other key attitudinal variables dealing with military life in Canada.

Further, if we incorporate into our discussion the various conceptual and empirical studies of the attitudinal morphology of Western military systems, the complexity of the issue of commitment in military life becomes more apparent. Consistently, studies have shown a bifurcation in attitudinal orientations toward military life, a pattern which is linked to the changing social context of military service.

Overall, there is a relatively high degree of thematic continuity in that literature.[16] Researchers and scholars have explored, over the past two decades, the theme of a fundamental division in attitudes toward the military and its institutional features among military personnel, calling into question the conventional image of value homogeneity among military personnel. The morphological distinctions raised by this research imply a fundamental cleavage between those for whom the military is an occupation in which they perform work, but without any appreciable commitment to the institution over the longer term, and those for whom it is not such an occupation. Within this theme, different analysts have emphasized different aspects, but all question the assumption of value homogeneity, varying only in degree, rather than type. Individuals in uniform do not share the same assumptions—there are those who are willing to enter combat and those who are not, those who grant status to the operational soldier and those who do not, those who emphasize the performance of duty regardless of specialization and those who focus on their occupational specialty, those who have internal reference groups and those with external reference groups, those who believe that role obligations for military personnel are not time limited and those who claim a private life away from the military institution, and those who focus on combat and battle and those who refuse to accept the operational focus. These attitudinal dimensions, which imply different worldviews on military service are linked together, with individuals lying on a continuum of commitment to traditional military values.[17]

I suggest here that the social reality of commitment patterns in military systems must be a matter of institutional concern. How members define military service and its inherent obligations and how they react, both individually and collectively, to organizational characteristics must continually be on the institutional agenda for military leaders and managers. Further, we must attempt conceptual precision, getting past the relatively facile, perhaps trivial, generalizations regarding commitment and its strategic importance in the longer run. Leaders at all levels of the military must be sensitive to that requirement.

LEADERS MUST BE SENSITIVE TO THAT CONCERN

That leaders in military systems, especially at the officer level, must be themselves committed is not at issue here. For the most part, leaders are attached to, and identify with, the norms of service in the military captured in the vocational definition of participation. This is clearly supported in my research into Army value orientations.[18] Unpublished data from a study of Canadian officers generally reflect a vocational orientation to military life at the officer level across all environments and classifications. But personal commitment is not enough: leaders must be sensitive to the need for commitment as an organizational characteristic and to the complex subtle implications of differences in type and intensity. Moreover, a critical and neglected aspect of their professional competence is their ability to create and sustain commitment, particularly at lower levels, through personal example and organizational design.

The later prescription is the main theme in George Strother's important article "The Moral Codes of Executives: A Watergate Inspired Look at Barnard's Theory of Executive Responsibility."[19] Strother examines Barnard's major writings in the context of the Watergate experience, and he notes that Barnard wrote about two fundamental aspects of leadership: technical competence and moral responsibility. In Strother's view, most analysts have seriously misrepresented Barnard's work because they have focused on the first aspect, the technical management of resources, in a rational way, but have almost completely neglected the second aspect, which deals directly with the intangible issue of organizational morale. Strother writes:

Barnard caps his description of executive responsibility with the view that responsible conformity to a complex set of codes is not enough at the highest executive levels. The effective executive must have the capacity to create moral codes for others. In this perspective, organizational morale is a manifestation of the success of the executive in creating commonly held codes within the organization (p. 16).

In other words, executives (leaders) are responsible for, and should be judged accordingly, on the criterion of organizational morale and the internalization of moral codes by members. Strother then goes on to postulate that commitment of members will rise in tandem with this executive capability.

This frame of reference is implicit in historic military culture: officers are morally responsible for organizational (unit) morale and are accountable for the commitment of their subordinates. Thus, in this frame of reference, the blame for a crisis of, say, the military ethos must be laid at the feet of the officer corps, because its collective responsibility is to generate moral codes for members. Blame, of course, is a radically different notion than cause, and we must not confuse the two, as Savage and Gabriel have done in *Crisis in Command*.[20] At the same time, it is appropriate to lay out as an agenda item for military leaders the responsibility factor for organizational morale in the sense conveyed by Strother's discussion. In peacetime, it is very difficult to know when officers have fallen short on criteria of professional effectiveness,[21] but I believe that this dimension is one which deserves more critical and systematic attention.

We must also go beyond the level of individual leaders to think about the ability of officers to create institutional characteristics which increase commitment, rather than detract from it. It is not enough to have leadership by example, for officers to set moral standards by their dress and deportment: they must also develop policies and institutional features that strengthen commitment. This is, of course, a more complex area, but much of the critical analysis to do with the military in North America has centered on the institutional level of analysis. Discussions of training, rotation policies, leadership instability, the military ethos, and rewards, among other things, are all linked to whether institutional policies are contributing to, or are eroding, commitment in the military. Thus those who energetically work, whether consciously or unconsciously, to reinforce the military as bureaucracy may in fact be undermining institutional effectiveness. History has shown that there are effective and ineffective ways of leading military members and of organizing their life environments, and that these ways bear upon the development and stabilization of commitment. We neglect that historical knowledge base at our peril. Officers, especially, must go beyond a rhetorical concern with commitment to examine institutional dynamics. This may require critical self-analysis, and I shall return to this point at the end of the chapter.

ALTHOUGH THE CONCEPT OF ORGANIZATIONAL COMMITMENT IS OF USE IN THE DESCRIPTIVE AND PRESCRIPTIVE ANALYSIS OF MILITARY POLICIES, IT HAS LIMITATIONS BECAUSE OF THE UNIQUE NATURE OF MILITARY GOALS

One of the most productive and systematic approaches to the study of organizational membership and participation is that centering around the concept of employee commitment using the Organizational Commitment Questionnaire.[22] This research vein is a rich one from both conceptual and epistemic viewpoints, particularly as it relates to the antecedents, correlates, and outcomes of organizational commitment. It has considerable relevance, through extrapolation, to important issues related to the manning of an all volunteer military. This is particularly the case in the context of concern with attrition and retention of members. Research on the Canadian military, for example, has shown that tenure after training among nonofficers is related to levels of organizational commitment.[23]

Although this line of analysis and research seems to be comparatively more systematic and rigorous than much of organizational analysis, it is limited in its direct applicability to the issues of military participation and effectiveness. The levels and type of commitment desired in the military are somewhat different than those required, or deemed desirable, in the great majority of civilian organizations where people are contractually limited employees. In the military, the organizational expectation is for extremely high levels of commitment and personal involvement with the minimum being the high end of scales such as the OCQ validated in civilian settings. In fact, commitment indicators in the context of the Canadian military suggest that there is a restriction of range problem in the upper end of the commitment continuum. Just about everyone scores high on the measures.

The problem may be with the measure and thus, ultimately, with the construct that underlies it. If the military is concerned with whether members, particularly in key operational roles, are committed until death, then we need measures that somehow tap into that unlimited liability, not the rather mundane and nondangerous civilian variety. The commitments of the firing line are rather different than those of the assembly line, and somehow we must tap into that central institutional concern. The errors, if one can use that term, are those of ommission rather than commission.

We need to be concerned with how organizational commitment relates to basic definitions of military service and its inherent role obligations. In other words, we have to join together the research and conceptualization on employee commitment to organizations with that exploring the normative nature of military service, seen as a *sui generis* form of activity. A purely nomothetic approach simply will not do as we cannot extrapolate from civilian to military settings, without taking into account the unique demands of the military and how members react to them. This is not to deny that there is a relationship between measures of organizational commitment and measures of vocational and occupational military orientations. In a study of the Canadian Army, the statistical relationship between commitment to the Canadian Forces as an organization and military ethos values was .52, with 1,667 respondents from all rank levels.[24] The relationship is positive and rather high, given the statistical properties of such research, but there are areas of significant ambiguity.

This ambiguity is highlighted in Table 4.1, which presents unpublished data from a sample of Canadian Forces officers, collected in tandem with the study of Army values noted earlier. Only captains (n = 388) are represented in this table to minimize any confounding effect from rank level. The respondents are broken down by latent role types of soldier, ambivalent, and employee using the Military Ethos Scale values outlined in a recent *Armed Forces and Society* article.[25] Soldiers are those with a clear vocational orientation toward military life, who score in the upper third of the scale; ambivalents are in the middle third; and employees are those with a clear occupational orientation toward military life, who score in the bottom third of the scale. Although the numbers in each category reflect the preponderance of vocational orientations among officers, this is not of interest here. (The original categories were developed using a larger sample of all serving ranks in the army.) Our concern is with the patterns of agreement, neutrality, and disagreement— expressed as percentage distributions—among role types on one of the items for the OCQ included in the survey. Original responses have been collapsed into three valence categories, with agreement with the statement "Often I find it difficult to agree with Forces' policies on important matters relating to its members" indicating lower or weaker organizational commitment.

One is mindful here that this is only one item in a fifteen-item scale, and the intent is not to question the overall scale, only to use it as a way of pointing up some of the ambiguities when we make linkages between attitudinal measures of organizational commitment and the context of member perceptions within the military. For our purposes here, we can see the tendencies in the distributions which would produce a statistical relationship on the order of .52, but the important information is the fact that fully a third of the soldier respondents answered in a manner (agreement) that indicates weak organizational commitment.

The reasons for the data distributions in Table 4.1 came out in the group interviews which accompanied administration of the survey instrument. Those with soldier orientations who agreed with the statement did so because they perceived the military's personnel policies to be too "civilianized" and not tough enough; those with employee orientations who agreed

Table 4.1
Attitudes toward Forces' Policies among Captains in the Officer Corps Sample, by Latent Role Type

"Often I find it difficult to agree with Forces' policies on important matters relating to its members."

Latent Role	Percent Agreeing	Percent Neutral	Percent Disagreeing	Total	N
Soldier	34.3	19.0	46.7	100.0	210
Ambivalent	34.1	22.7	43.2	100.0	141
Employee	67.6	8.1	24.3	100.0	37
TOTAL	37.3	19.3	43.3	100.0	388

with the statement did so because they found the present organizational style too "militarized" and too tough—similar response categories in both cases but with completely different logics and viewpoints. The quantitative data would suggest convergent views and organizational commitment levels, but nothing could be farther from the truth. The soldiers are committed to a radical model of military life, and their commitment to the military *qua* institution is, in fact, radical in its intensity. Both groups, however, are weakly committed to the organization as they perceive it to *be*, but this does not tell the full institutional story, unless we go past the responses to get into the meanings of the actors involved and set these in the broader context of the changing character of military organization.

The criteria by which we evaluate individual and systematic effectiveness in the military are, of course, subject to debate. In certain contexts of policy formation and discussion, the organizational commitment of members has relevance as a dependent variable in analysis, but I would argue that its use is limited if we do not link it to the range of institutional concerns examined in recent books such as Sarkesian's *Combat Effectiveness* and Kellett's *Combat Motivation*.[26] At some point, one must identify the bottom line for institutional analysis, to borrow a term from the world of entrepreneurial capitalism. In my view, as long as operations are the payoff, we must be concerned with the operational commitment, *the will to fight*, of military participants.

At the same time, however, the findings from the systematic research into organizational commitment bear noting by military planners. Of special relevance are those factors which Steers, Mowday, and Porter term the "work experience correlates of commitment."[27] These are the work experiences which are "a major socializing force and as such represent an important influence on the extent to which psychological attachments are formed with the organization" (p. 19). The ones which are, in my view, of considerable military relevance are *organizational dependability*, or the extent to which employees feel the organization can be depended upon to look after their interests; *personal feelings of importance to the organization*, when employees feel they are needed and relevant to the organization's mission; *met expectations*, when employees feel their expectations are met by the organization; the *positive pro-organizational attitudes of coworkers*, those environmental sentiments which rub off on people; and *social involvement*, which produces stronger social ties and greater involvement in the life of the organization, so that it becomes a central life interest of the individuals concerned.

Anyone familiar with the military literature on cohesion, officer ethics, leadership, effectiveness, and military socialization within the defense community will immediately see the import of these factors and how they converge with traditional military thought. These, it seems to me, are the vital ingredients long recognized as important in developing the key intangible of morale. The linkages, in other words, are there, between research on organizational commitment and the central institutional concerns of the military. I am struck by the way in which the factors discussed in organizational commitment research articulate with the underlying agenda of military analysts such as Savage and Gabriel, Moskos, and Kellett. The crucial requirement is to make the articulation explicit: to link military postulates regarding cohesion, trust, and reciprocity between leaders—as organizational representatives—and followers and the nature of the military as an institution to findings such as those listed above. Without that articulation, the differences in terminology will obscure the connections. In Canada, at least, members of the military are not yet called employees, and the use of that term can put a very quick stop to potentially fruitful discussion.

IT IS DANGEROUS AND THREATENING TO ANALYZE COMMITMENT BECAUSE THE ENEMY MAY BE OURSELVES

To analyze is, in one sense, to admit that one's beliefs have been shaken, that what one once saw clearly is now seen through a glass darkly. In a recent article in the *Canadian Defence Quarterly*, I argued that military officers are not given to introspection on the nature of their vocation to the state and on the underlying assumptions of that vocation.[28] In this perspective, one is reminded of the old military adage that it is dangerous for the soldier to do too much thinking on the nature of his metier. I am not so sure that it is, in the present context, dangerous, but it can be threatening to one's images of self and the current institutional character of the military. Valued cultural images may founder on the shoals of current reality. As Morris Janowitz noted in *The Professional Soldier*: "The military is no longer an isolated calling functioning to protect the honor of society; it is now a profession subject to all the vicissitudes of careerism in a bureaucratic setting."[29] If we take this as a reasonably accurate assessment of the situation now, and I believe this to be the case, then the contextual difficulties in the analysis of commitment come into focus. The central cultural themes of the military through history are not those of bureaucratic intrigue, but of the "isolated calling functioning to protect the honor of society." Thus there is a disjunction between culture and structure which creates dissonance at the individual level.

To see ourselves as we are—officers in particular—rather than how we ought to be, threatens valued and important self-conceptions. This is the threatening aspect referred to in the reflection above. We may be forced to confront the fact that we and our institution have not lived up to our own expectations. Thus it is easier to objectify the issue or to put one's head in the proverbial sand. This, though, is the last thing that should happen with the officer corps. As Downey puts the matter in *Management in the Armed Forces*: "The military is perhaps second only to religion in the extent to which in peace it must question its tenets and beliefs: in war it is second to none in its need for strong, easily interpreted doctrine."[30] However threatening, however psychologically difficult, then, the process of institutional introspection might be, it is necessary. The danger, though, is that we may in fact discover that we have failed, since the officer corps is the architect of the military institution. If it lacks the mechanisms to generate commitment, then the responsibility is our own, and we have denied our calling.

There is, too, another danger inherent in the systematic analysis of commitment in military settings: we may find that our cherished assumptions are not grounded in fact, that commitment does not really matter, or that it cannot be controlled. Analysis is a rational process, yet commitment and combat motivation may be irrational. What if, as the result of very systematic research, we discover that our myths—the central cultural themes of military life—have little or no truth value? What then?

Perhaps we should leave well enough alone and accept Donovan's point that "the most inspiring creeds and noble codes of fighting men are universal, ancient, and unquestioned."[31] As an article of faith, I am inclined to agree with it, but I believe that there is a requirement in the turbulent modern context for sincere questioning. What the military needs more than ever, and what the officer corps must provide, is that dynamic quality which the scholastics termed *fides quarens intellectum*, "faith seeking understanding." We need military philosophy to give us a clear grasp of values and organizational science to give us a grasp of techniques, for without both we shall continue to muddle through the process of institution building in the military.

NOTES

1. James Fallows, *National Defense* (New York: Random House, 1981), p. 171. This is one of the more insightful and comprehensive assessments of the American defense system. Of particular concern in this chapter are those sections that deal with military values and the changing nature of military service.

2. See Charles Moskos, "The Emergent Military: Civil, Traditional, or Plural," *Pacific Sociological Review* 6 (1973), pp. 255–80, and "From Institution to Occupation: Trends in Military Organization," *Armed Forces and Society* (Fall 1977), pp. 41–51.

3. P.G. Donnelly, C.A. Cotton, and E.C. Tierney, *Factors Affecting the Stay/Leave Decision of Post Pay Level 3 Graduates*, Working Paper 80–1 (Toronto, Ontario: Canadian Forces Personnel Applied Research Unit, 1980).

4. Charles Cotton, "The Divided Army: Role Orientations among Canada's Peacetime Soldiers," Ph.D. diss., Carleton University, Ottawa, Ontario, 1980. This research is also reported in *Military Attitudes and the Values of the Army in Canada*, Research Report 79–5 (Toronto, Ontario: Canadian Forces Personnel Applied Research Unit, 1979, and "Institutional and Occupational Values in Canada's Army," *Armed Forces and Society* 8, no. 1 (Fall 1981), pp. 99–110, by the same author.

5. E.E. Cummings, "The Importance of Processes and Contexts in Organizational Psychology," paper presented at a symposium on Industrial/Organizational Psychology Research, annual meeting of the

American Psychological Association, Montreal, Canada, September 3, 1980.

6. Ibid., p. 16.

7. The term "myth" is used here in a technical sense to refer to the central cultural themes and "stories" that pervade a particular organizational or group culture. This is the sense in which I take it to be used by Cummings in "The Importance of Processes and Contexts."

8. Richard M. Steers, Richard T. Mowday, and Lyman W. Porter, *Employee Commitment to Organizations: A Conceptual Review*, Technical Report No. 7, (Eugene: University of Oregon, Graduate School of Management, August 1981). Prepared under Office of Naval Research Contract N00014–K–0026, this is a significant review paper on the topic and an important source of bibliographic material. It is unfortunate that analysts dealing with the military as a substantive focus have not incorporated the perspectives and findings contained in this paper into their work. It seems that there are "two solitudes" in this case: one dealing with organizational commitment as a nomothetic issue and the other dealing with military role orientations as an ideographic issue.

9. See, for example, Sam C. Sarkesian, ed., *Combat Effectiveness* (Beverly Hills, Calif.: Sage Publications, 1980), and Anthony Kellett, *Combat Motivation* (Boston: Kluwer Nijhoff, 1982) for introductions to this field.

10. Marion J. Levy, "Armed Force Organizations," in *The Military and Modernization*, ed. Henry Bienen (New York: Aldine Atherton, 1971), p. 59.

11. "Cohesion and Disintegration in the Wehrmacht in World War II." Recently reprinted in Morris Janowitz, *Military Conflict* (Beverly Hills, Calif.: Sage Publications, 1975), pp. 177–220.

12. J.C.T. Downey, *Management in the Armed Forces: An Anatomy of the Military Profession* (London: McGraw-Hill, 1977), p. 62. This book is one of the best analytical treatments of officership and defense organization in modern industrial democracies.

13. Sir John Hackett, "Today and Tomorrow," in *War, Morality and the Military Profession*, ed. M. Wakin (Boulder, Colo.: Westview Press, 1979), p. 101. Hackett's words capture better than most the timeless nature of the soldier's calling: "The essential basis of military life is the ordered application of force under an unlimited liability."

14. Morris Janowitz discusses this point at some length in the revised prologue to the 2nd edition of *The Professional Soldier* (New York: Free Press, 1971).

15. Unpublished data from the research into military values and attitudes of serving personnel in Canada's army from Cotton, "The Divided Army." For a discussion of the correlations between the

dimensions of Canadian military values, see pages 71 to 74 (Table 12) in Cotton, *Military Attitudes and Values of the Army in Canada,* and Table 3 in Cotton, "Institutional and Occupational Values in Canada's Army."

16. The material is discussed at length in Chapter 11 of Cotton, "The Divided Army."

17. Table 3 in Cotton, "Institutional and Occupational Values in Canada's Army," presents data on many of these attitudinal aspects of how military service is defined.

18. Table 2 in Cotton, "Institutional and Occupational Values in Canada's Army," shows that the great majority of leaders in Army settings have institutional orientations.

19. George Strother, "The Moral Codes of Executives: A Watergate Inspired Look at Barnard's Theory of Executive Responsibility," *Academy of Management Review* (April 1976), pp. 13–22.

20. Paul Savage and Richard Gabriel, *Crisis in Command* (New York: Hill and Wang, 1978). On this point, see Charles Cotton, "A Canadian View of the United States Army," *Armed Forces and Society* 3 (May 1977), pp. 475–80.

21. See, for example, the discussions in the anthology edited by Sarkesian, *Combat Effectiveness.* Of special relevance to this point is the work of Lewis Sorley: "Prevailing Criteria: A Critique," Chapter 2 in the Sarkesian volume, and "Competence as Ethical Imperative: Issues of Professionalism," Chapter 3 in *Military Ethics and Professionalism,* ed. J. Brown and M. Collins, Essay Series 81–2 (Washington, D.C.: National Defense University, 1981).

22. The basic reference is that by Steers, Mowday, and Porter, *Employee Commitment.*

23. Donnelly, Cotton, and Tierney, *Factors Affecting the Stay/Leave Decision.*

24. Cotton, *Military Attitudes and the Values of the Army in Canada,* Table 12.

25. Cotton, "Institutional and Occupational Values in Canada's Army," pp. 105–8.

26. Sarkesian, *Combat Effectiveness,* and Kellett, *Combat Motivation.*

27. Steers, Mowday, and Porter, *Employee Commitment,* pp. 19–20.

28. Charles Cotton, "A Canadian Military Ethos," *Canadian Defence Quarterly* 12, no. 3 (Winter 1982/83), pp. 10–18.

29. Janowitz, *The Professional Soldier,* p. xii.

30. Downey, *Management in the Armed Forces,* p. 134.

31. James Donovan, *Militarism USA* (New York: Charles Scribner's Sons, 1970), p. xx.

PART II

Sources of Legitimacy and Commitment

Following an initial description and analysis of the interrelationships between the main concepts involved, the second part of this volume focuses on the sources—whether profluent and clear, or limited and ambiguous—of legitimacy and commitment. Frederick Manning and David Marlowe, representing an interdisciplinary combination of social psychology, psychiatry, and anthropology, propose three main sources of legitimacy for soldiers' acts of violence: societal sources, ethical codes, and small-group factors. By delineating these sources in an historical perspective, the authors educate us on the trends and changes in the relative weights of the different sources. Their review concludes with a rather skeptical prospective regarding future wars.

Conscientious objection can serve as a most interesting example of an existing conflict between legitimacy and commitment. Most conscientious objectors are highly committed individuals, who do not accept the causes of wars—any war—as legitimate ones. Their commitment is to their own values and norms, not to those of the state. Accordingly, Charles Moskos analyzes conscientious objection to military service from a dual point of view: that of the individual and that of the state. Moskos, who is a world-known military sociologist, extends this analysis across groups and religious congregations as well as along historical stages, which are roughly related to the industrial revolution.

The author of Chapter 7, Eugene Weiner, is an Israeli sociologist who has served in several of Israel's wars and has dealt with many bereaved families. Weiner deals with the most critical and painful price of war legitimacy, that is, the price of war casualties.

Questions about the legitimacy of war begin when doubts about the worthwhileness of the sacrifice of the fallen soldiers not only intrude into the mourning families, but also become a public issue. While describing the special characteristics of the Israeli society and of the Jewish traditions in mourning and bereavement, the author unravels the intricate mechanisms by which the military procedures neutralize the personal family distress and reinforce the "institutional" aspects of the mourning process. Hence, the risk of losing legitimacy for future wars, with their additional casualties, is prevented, or at least minimized.

It becomes quite apparent that types of commitment as well as sources of legitimacy may alter according to "national singularities" and "varying social histories" (in Moskos' terms). The chapters in this section illuminate some of these alterations along cultural groups and historical periods.

5

The Legitimation of Combat for the Soldier

Frederick J. Manning and David H. Marlowe

The issue of the legitimacy of war and killing has been a significant human concern for millenia. Human groups have not generally regarded the taking of life as an issue to be dealt with lightly. All societies have well-defined boundaries outside of which acts of both social and individual violence are formally prohibited. For almost all there is also a body of law, custom, or belief that redefines the fundamental prohibitions against ingroup violence in such ways as to approve the violence of combat. Through much of human history and within almost all human societies, the question of the legitimacy of war and combat has been a matter of cultural consensus. Legitimacy for the soldier (i.e., the conviction that he is acting correctly in killing others of his kind) was attained by behaving according to the rules and expectations laid down by his culture and society.

The thesis of this chapter is that soldiers' acts of violence are legitimized by rules and expectations from three powerful sources: society as a whole, the soldier/warrior ethic, and the small fighting group. That is, soldiers are allowed, encouraged, even obligated to kill because of their duties as citizens, duties as soldiers, and duties as comrades. These duties provide the soldier with his reasons for both killing and risking his own life. They provide his conviction that he is right to fight. These three duties are only partially overlapping. They affect the soldier at different times and in different situations—citizenship, for example, may influence enlistment far more than it affects actual fighting, where small-group and soldier ethic pressures are more relevant—and in recent years their intercorrelation has diminished considerably, at least in Western nations. This uncoupling has produced crises for both soldiers and societies and does not seem likely to correct itself in the near future.

SOCIETAL FACTORS

A multiplicity of mechanisms exists to ensure the soldier's sense of legitimacy in societies without centralized sociopolitical organizations. Here the military force truly embodies and represents the group. The armed forces is neither a specialized, permanently dedicated segment of the group nor a symbolic representation of it—it is the group itself. In societies such as the Somali, in which the military group, all males between the ages of sixteen and sixty, is inseparable from the rest of the social system, duties as citizen, as soldier, and as comrade are interlocked. Reliable participation in battle and the effectiveness of the individual in combat lay in those same norms—the reciprocal rights, duties, and obligations of kin to each other—that maintained the overall ordering of the society. The decision to make war is in response to societal perceptions defining the situation as one in which warfare is a licit response. The Somali as a warrior people are sensitive and responsive to the wide range of insults and injuries that might require a violent response and that might be construed as cause for compensation, feud, or war. Their response is in fact shaped by a variety of other factors, the most important of which is the degree of real or fictive kin relationship between the injury-giving and the injured groups. An assault inflicted by a member of a different clan is seen and referred to as an act of war and leads immediately to preparation for armed combat. A more serious offense, which takes place within the clan, is usually seen as a bad thing but not as a *causus belli*. The response then is negotiation for compensation without individual or organized violence. Thus, when a clan member was assaulted and beaten with a camel stick by a member of another clan, externally imposed police intervention was required to prevent an outbreak of serious warfare. When a fight between members of two lineages within the same clan took place, one that left eight men seriously wounded, it was referred to as an accident and all the injured and their kinsmen agreed that any quest for vengeance or retaliation was not allowable. To help preclude any thought of vengeance, acts of assault committed within the group were considered to be the product of aberrant or mentally ill behavior on the part of the perpetrator. In one specific case, an old woman was gravely assaulted and raped by a distant member of her own lineage. She specifically enjoined her sons and close kinsmen from initiating a violent response or a quest for vengeance, saying that, "This man is of our lineage. You shall not give him to the police nor shall you seek to kill him. The blood of a 'brother' does not take away my blood." One of her nephews noted, "[T]he man who did this thing. We know him well. . . . He is a little bit crazy. I think maybe he saw a Djinn once and it makes him act that way. . . . We are very angry. We want him punished but it is not a thing we should make war or kill over." Although traditional Somali culture encourages violence as the preferred means of response in all situations in which a violent offense has been committed, the need to maintain intragroup harmony and boundaries demands and achieves both gross and subtle reorganization of the value of violence-evoking stimuli. These boundaries define the legitimacy of participation in armed combat for the warrior.

Armies are social groups' ultimate mode of maintaining the necessary and desired ordering of their universe. Until quite recently the legitimacy of an act of war made by the state might be questioned by its citizens, but the propriety of its military forces in carrying out the act was seldom queried. That is, the issue of the legitimacy of the soldier's engagement in combat did not excite past observers and commentators nearly as much as did the issue of the legitimacy of war itself or of specific acts of war. The Melian dialogue, for example, perhaps the most widely known argument from classical times on the legitimacy of an act of war, argues only the legitimacy of Athens making war upon Melos. The dialogue contrasts the justice of a cause (Melos) with the doctrine of might serving its own ends (Athens).[1] At no point in the dialogue is the legitimacy of the action taken by the military force in the performance of its mission brought into question. The proper order of things in ancient Greece lay in the will of the gods, and the armies of both sides worked out that will, which was determined by the outcome.

In this view, the soldier was never perceived as having an ethical choice about his commitment to battle. The legitimacy of his military acts flowed from the absolute subordination of the soldier to the state and thence to the gods or to God. Legitimacy lay in the faithful performance of one's duty, not in personally weighing the merits of every action. The soldier was thus entitled to say, as one does in Henry V: "We know enough if we know we are the king's men. Our obedience to the king wipes the crime of it out of us."[2]

This perception of war and of each act of combat as an expression of divine will was probably the major contextual element that defined the legitimacy of his occupation for the soldier of ancient times. In Western as well as a number of other traditions this is underlined by the quasi-sacred nature attributed to armies and to soldiers as those members of society who are licensed, as Dumezeil[3] has said of the warrior, to "know sin." The soldier is expected to shed blood and to take life—to carry out the will of God as a master of life and death.

In the Old Testament, Levitical injunctions demonstrate this identification with divine will in the rituals that were to be observed in the military camp, the carrying of the Ark of the Convenant into battle, and the polluting aspects of bloodshed and the taking of life. In the Greek polis, war was even more sacral in nature. Burkett[4] says that, for the Greek city state, war "may almost appear like one great sacrificial action." There were preliminary offerings, sacrificial offerings made on the battlefield, and vows made before and during the battle. Each battle was dedicated and sworn to the patron gods of the polis by the participants. The contingencies associated with ritual attempted to guarantee the combat performance of the participants, not only indirectly, by enhancing cohesion and esprit, but also directly, by making withdrawal from battle on the part of any soldier who did not wish to fight the commission of blasphemy. The penalty was to be stoned to death. This enmeshing of the soldier in the performance of the will of God, embodied in the institutions of the state, is seen most powerfully in the oath taken by recruits to the Roman Legions following the Christianization of the Roman Empire as reported by Vegetius:

They swear by God, by Christ and by the Holy Ghost; and by the majesty of the Emperor who, after God, should be the chief object of the love and veneration of mankind. For when he has received the title of August, his subjects are bound to pay him the most sincere devotion and homage, as the representative of God on earth. And every man, whether in a private or military station, serves God who serves him faithfully who reigns by His authority. The soldiers also swear they will obey the Emperor willingly and implicitly in all his commands, that they will never desert and will always be ready to sacrifice their lives for the Roman Empire.[5]

Much later Machiavelli described this vision of obedience to one's commanders and leaders in a far less noble but more pragmatic fashion. Soldiers hold in their hands the lever of physical power by which the state or their social group and its political leadership may live or die, endure or pass away. Their loyalty and fealty as well as their competence and capacity to perform their mandated tasks are always central to the maintenance and security of the governing body of the state. The social order defined by any political authority is, as a matter of course, at risk from any armed force, including its own. Machiavelli saw that the religious oath of the Romans was needed, "because to control armed men the fear neither of the laws nor of men is enough. The ancients added to them the authority of God; and therefore with great ceremonies they had their soldiers swear to observe military discipline, in order that if they acted against it, they would have to fear not merely the laws and men but God; and they used every device to give them strong religious feeling."[6]

Subordination to God and the state was not the only legitimation of the soldier's participation in combat. Participation and commitment are guaranteed and combat legitimated by the demands of role and status in secular society as well as by religious obligation. This is clearly defined by the god Krishna for the warrior prince Arjuna in the *Bhagavad-Gita*:

If you refuse to fight this righteous war, you will be turning aside from your duty. You will be a sinner and disgraced. People will speak ill of you throughout the ages. To a man who values his honor, that is surely worse than death. The warrior chiefs believe that it was fear that drove you from the battle; you will be despised by those that have admired you so long. Your enemies also will slander your courage. They will use the words which should never be spoken. What could be harder to bear than that.[7]

MILITARY-ETHICAL FACTORS

The legitimation of combat and battle derived from what might be called the "way of the warrior" also has a long history. Homer saw the warrior as held to his task not by the Ionic equivalent of an evoked *furor celticus* or *teutonicus* but by the need to maintain the public status and obligations incurred by being a member of a warrior caste. Witness the well-known speech of Sarpedon to Glaucus in Book XII of Homer's *Iliad*:

Why hold we a great grant-farm by the banks of Xanthus Fair with orchard and corn-rich plow-land?
For this: that we now with the foremost Lycians
Must stand and exchange the blows of searing battle
So that one may say, some Lycian with his armor:
They are not so fameless that rule in Lycia
These Kings of ours, that eat the fattened flocks
With the honey sweet choice wine. It seems their force
Is good, since they fight with the foremost Lycians.
Sweet fool, if only escaping this one war
We two would be able, ageless, immortal,
To live, then I'd neither fight with the foremost
Nor would I send you a battle that wins reknown.[8]

This source of legitimacy assumed greater importance in Western societies as military bodies began to evolve as distinct from civil government. In later classical times, specialists fulfilled the roles of general; the role was no longer simply another aspect of political leadership. Generals were lent and borrowed, and mercenary forces began to play an expanded role in both wars with the Persians and wars amongst the Greeks. Some soldiers were hirelings, mercenaries who served solely for pay, not out of the obligations of citizenship; others were professional generals who moved from state to state.[9] Recruitment, the relationship of the hireling-soldier to committed service, and the legitimacy of fighting the state's battles developed as major issues. The Romans also wrestled with these issues. Machiavelli still later dealt with them as central issues in *On the Art of War*, *The Discourses*, and *The Prince*, distinguishing the performance of those who serve for the wage from those who serve as citizens of the state or republic.[10] Machiavelli pointed out instance after instance in which the primary motive of money was not enough that mercenary forces would actually consider risking their lives in defense of their patrons and employers.

Perhaps in response to this problem, both premodern and modern armies have provided, within their tactical doctrine and their organization of combat forces, systems designed to provide high levels of support and to ensure the soldier's commitment to battle. Honor, bravery, and discipline were made the touchstones of soldiering, the standards of manhood. Nowhere was this more explicit than in the Europe of the Middle Ages, where chivalry governed not only the conduct of war, but the whole of noble life. Developed at the time of the great crusades of the twelfth century as a code intended to bring the fighting man into harmony with Christian doctrine, it flourished, at least in part, because of a variety of political and technological developments in "German Europe" following the fall of Rome. Chivalry signaled the reemergence of fighting as the province of the elite. Smaller and smaller kingdoms meant smaller and smaller armies and an increased dependence upon individual skills as opposed to cohesive masses. The size of armies, even in proportion to the much smaller populations of the medieval world, was impressively small. Hale[11] points out that the largest forces deployed to France from England in the Hundred Years War was 32,000 men and that few battles were fought with more than 15,000. New and expensive armor and weaponry also hastened the development of a warrior class. White, for example, has pointed to the stirrup in this regard.[12] An innovation of the early feudal period, the stirrup in combination with early forms of armor gave the mounted warrior much the same advantage over unmounted peasants and villagers as the tank had over the twentieth-century infantry. Such a shock effect did not come cheaply, however, and nonnobles came to play a smaller and smaller role in warfare. The ideal of chivalry in fact was a vision of order and justice maintained by a warrior class. The noble's distinguishing feature was the practice of arms. He was supposed to protect the people from oppression, combat tyranny, and cultivate virtue—and, in return, he was spared the taxation that was the lot of the peasant and the townsman. Prowess—a combination of courage, strength, and skill—was an essential requirement of the chevalier, but honor and loyalty were the ideals. At a time when a pledge between lord and vassal was the only form of government, a knight who broke his oath was charged with treason for betraying the order of knighthood. Chivalry thus created a universal order of all Christian knights, a transnational class moved by a single ideal, a military guild in which all knights were theoretically brothers.[13] In practice they fell far short of their ideals, but the notion of a brotherhood in arms, marked by bravery, honor, and loyalty, survived the eventual demise of the armored knight and the revival of the infantry as the queen of battle. The Saxon-Polish Field Service Rules of 1752 illustrates this:

For the officer, honor is reserved, for the common man obedience and loyalty. . . . From honor flows intrepidity and equanimity in danger, zeal to win ability and experience, respect for superiors, modesty towards one's equals, condescension toward inferiors. . . . Nothing therefore must incite the officer but honor, which carries its own recompense; but the soldier is driven and restrained and educated to discipline by reward and fear. . . . The worst soldier is an officer without honor, a common man without discipline.[14]

The reemergence of large nations and mass armies undermined the real basis of chivalry—the identification of warfare with nobility—and other mechanisms for ensuring enthusiastic participation came to the fore once more. These mechanisms were coercion and the interpersonal bonds of the primary group. Neither of these was new to warfare. Gibbon, for example, described discipline in the Roman Army: "It was impossible for cowardice or disobedience to escape the severest punishment. The centurions were authorized to chastise with blows, the generals had a right to punish with death; and it was an inflexible maxim of Roman discipline that a good soldier should dread his officers far more than the enemy."[15]

Seventeenth-century armies were in many respects far more similar to those of the fourth century than to those of the fourteenth. To supplement mercenary forces, conscriptees were dragooned, shanghaied, ensnared, and enrolled by force.[16] Criminals, the urban poor, and landless laborers often found themselves swept up by recruiting impressment teams. Since they were neither contractual professionals like the standing mercenary cadres of armies, nor vested maintainers of status like the minor service nobilities and gentry, legitimation did not come with the role of soldier and warrior. The conscriptee, often unwilling, sometimes recalcitrant, at times criminal, and seldom benefitting from his service, was taught another version of legitimacy, coercion and force. Typified best perhaps by the policies of Frederick the Great of Prussia, the soldiers of levied armies learned that there was more to fear from not performing their duty at the desired level than from the enemy. Iron discipline, the order of the day, was enforced in garrison with the drumhead court martial and in war with the arbitrary power of life and death allocated to noncommissioned officers and officers.

SMALL-GROUP FACTORS

In practice, effective premodern military units relied not only upon discipline, but also upon the support and coherence provided their members by being a part of an organized group. Soldiers drew strength, security, and a sense of invulnerability from the physical presence of the "line," from the shoulder-to-shoulder contact with their fellows. Their confidence and sense of competence were enhanced and extended by the drills and convolutions of their parade ground which made each a part of a powerful whole. The well-trained, well-disciplined soldier could submerge himself in the organism which was his company or the line of battle, marching, turning, moving, thrusting, parrying, discharging musketry as one mighty whole.

The psychological and moral integrity of the soldier was enormously dependent upon the maintenance of the physical integrity of the line of battle. If the line broke, the soldier was prone to break and to cease to be capable of effective performance in combat. The Roman Legion as described by Vegetius (A.D.) devoted its core training and built its organizational structure to ensure the functional integrity and indissolubility of the line of battle and its constituent groups. Vegetius describes as the most essential reason for drills to "teach soldiers to keep their ranks and never abandon their colors in the most difficult evolutions. Men thus trained are never at a loss amidst the greatest confusion of numbers." Indeed the maintenance of the line and of order was the primary concern of legionary infantry as Vegetius describes it.

The light armed troops . . . advanced in the front of the line and attacked the enemy. If they could make them give way, they pursued them; but if they were repulsed by superior bravery or numbers they retired behind their own heavy armed infantry, which appeared like a wall of iron and renewed the action, at first with their missile weapons then sword in hand. If they broke the enemy they never pursued them lest they should break their ranks or throw the line into confusion, and lest the enemy taking advantage of their disorder, should return to the attack and destroy them without difficulty.[17]

The physical bonding and ordering of drill was profoundly reinforced by the social ordering, group identification, and bonding of the legionnaires. Each legion was divided into ten cohorts, each with its unique ensign or "dragon," and each cohort was divided into ten centuries of a hundred men, each century with "an ensign inscribed with the number of both the cohort and century so that the men keeping it in sight might be prevented from separating from their comrades in the greatest tumults."[18] Each century was further divided into squads or messes or ten men under the command of a *decanus* (a commander of ten). These *conturbinia* or maniples who ate, lived, and marched together always fought together. In the Roman Legion, then, social organization, training, and tactics merged to reinforce each other to optimize the combat performance of the line of battle. This general model has been followed in formally constituted armies from classical times through World War I. Each small group was supposed to be strongly bonded and woven into the larger assault or defensive line of the company, battalion, or regimental front, an arrangement that upheld both the psychological integrity of the soldier and the solidarity of the line. This ordering provided operational and behavioral legitimacy to the soldier in combat. Decisions were made for the mass which moved in ranks and behaved, for the most part, in response to the orders given by the leadership. Legitimacy for the soldier was in a very real sense part of the organic and mechanical solidarity of the military organization itself. Through World War I, the soldier who attempted to evade combat or flee or who went to ground suffered the contempt and opprobrium of his group.

The heavy casualties among the assault troops of World War I made it painfully clear, however, that modern weapons had rendered obsolete the formations and tactics that had sustained soldiers and armies for the previous 2,000 years or more. Ardant DuPicq, who had actually seen this transformation coming late in the nineteenth century, argued not only that wider dispersion of troops on the battlefield would be necessary because of the accuracy and lethality of modern (1870) weapons against massed troops in the open, but further that dispersed formations would require a drastic and qualitative change in the way in which soldiers were motivated and controlled.[19] The phalanx, square, and line could not survive the accuracy of cannon fire, rifled barrels, and the machine gun.

The resulting emphasis on smaller, more independent, maneuverable units, culminating in today's fire teams of three or four soldiers, gave increasing importance to these units as goads, guides, and supports for soldier performance in combat. The survey research conducted throughout World War II by Stouffer and his colleagues,[20] the POW interrogations of Shils and Janowitz,[21] and the attempts of army psychiatrists to cope with an avalanche of psychiatric casualties[22] all reinforced the view that it was the small face-to-face group that set the standards of conduct and sustained and supported the modern soldier in combat. Advancing on the enemy was a result of concern for the opinion of the other members of the unit, of a desire to avoid letting the other fellow down,[23] or perhaps to avenge the death of a squadmate.[24] Commitment to an ideology, nation, or social-political system played only a small role in this view; it served primarily as a motivation for enlistment rather than a spur to actual fighting or an aid in enduring. In Baynes' words, "[T]he writer or speaker about war has more faith in causes than men who actually fight."[25]

As a motivational system, if we can use the term "system" for this largely spontaneous development of comradely ties among soldiers of the same squad or platoon, small-group cohesion is not without its drawbacks. Specifically, if the main inducement to fighting is that by so doing one is discharging a duty to the group, then one might logically expect enthusiastic fighting only when it is obvious that fighting is in the best interest of the group. It is no coincidence that "hero" has been a pejorative in the front lines during all the U.S. conflicts of this century. Ashworth has documented the widespread development of a live-and-let-live philosophy with accompanying ritualization of fighting during the latter half of World War I.[26] He argues that S.L.A. Marshall's famous finding that only 15 percent of soldiers ever fired their weapons in the average World War II firefight[27] should be seen in a similar light. Certainly Little noted that the longer a platoon was on the line in Korea, the more intensive the relationship of its members became, and the more their behavior deviated from the norms of the organization.[28] "The probable response," he says, "in executing orders in situations involving great risk was accordingly uncertain." When an organization reached this stage it was described as having "low morale" and withdrawn into reserve for "retraining." Paradoxically, the Nuremberg trials, which rang down the curtain on World War II, made it quite clear that however well an army could fight on the basis of intramilitary values alone (i.e., obeying orders and not letting friends down), these values were not sufficient legitimation, in the eyes of the victors at least, for any and all combat behaviors. If we may rely on statistics for a metaphor, small-group processes accounted for far more of the variance in World War II soldiers' fighting spirit than did commitment to societal ideals. Subsequent wars, to continue the statistical metaphor, suggest that this apparently small contribution of societal approval in World War II may well have been a result of a restricted range of societal views on the legitimacy of that war.

DISCREPANCIES

The Vietnam War and now Israel's experience in and after Lebanon have made it clear that soldiers and armies cannot fight effectively without a societal mandate. That is, legitimacy derived solely from within the military (honor, obedience, loyalty to the small group), though certainly necessary to sustain the soldier in combat, is not sufficient. Kirkland argues convincingly that the stunning defeat of the French Army by weaker forces in 1940, despite being forewarned, mobilized, trained, and deployed in strong defensive works, was in great measure traceable to the erosion of military values and standards by antimilitarism sentiments during the interwar period. In his words:

Popular repudiation of the military values of which the officer corps was the traditional custodian, and official toleration of this repudiation, compromised the fundamental ideological basis on which professional officers founded their identity. . . . Their response was to modify their group fantasy from forward-looking, tough-minded intellectualism to a myth oriented authoritarianism . . . [They] shied away from responsibility, avoided risk by conforming rigorously to regulation, endowed traditions with reality in preference to objective conditions, derogated members of other groups, reaffirmed fervently held values that came under challenge, ignored facts that did not fit into their preconceived world view, and urged adherence to procedure.[29]

In Korea, U.S. troops fought well, despite the introduction of an individual rotation system which, though well intentioned, did much to undermine the sustaining power of group identification. The stalemate resulting from the July 1953 armistice, however, provided the first indications that the small-group cohesion which had sustained combat performance in the heat of battle might be insufficient to sustain soldiers in the very different hostilities of the Cold War era. Unlike its 1918 predecessor, this armistice required the maintenance of large, fully armed, constantly alert forces trained, equipped, and poised to strike on a moment's notice. Food, shelter, sanitation, and recreation were much improved over prearmistice conditions, but they were still wretched by stateside standards and assumed greater importance in the absence of gunfire. Bonds to comrades and leaders formed by sharing dull and tedious duties were only pale copies of those forged in the heat of combat. Perhaps most important, it became difficult for soldiers to see a purpose in their activities, or inactivity, or in the continued need for discipline, physical fitness, and diligent maintenance of equipment. As a result, U.S. forces continued to suffer psychiatric casualties at a rate not much lower than the rates of the prior combat years, although the predominant symptoms changed from a paralyzing anxiety to apathy, depression, drug and alcohol abuse, and other forms of "character and behavior disorders."[30]

A related and far more serious phenomenon occurred in Vietnam in the five years following the Tet offensives of 1968. During this time, U.S. troops became increasingly relegated to support roles, as "Vietnamization" took place and opposition to the war grew louder and more widespread back home in America. The initials U.U.U.U.—the unwilling, led by the unqualified, doing the unnecessary, for the ungrateful—showed up in war zone graffiti as often as Kilroy had appeared in World War II. Drug use, racial disturbances, disciplinary infractions of all types, even attacks on superiors (fragging) grew steadily in base camps, and search-and-destroy missions in the jungle turned to "search and avoid" among soldiers determined not to be the last to die in Vietnam. Gabriel and Savage[31] argued that this collapse was due to the misbehavior and incompetence of the officer corps, and few would deny that "body counts" and other statistics were manipulated, club and PX funds embezzled, medals and glory inequitably distributed, war crimes covered up, and incompetent leaders allowed to squander lives through abbreviated commands for career purposes. None of this is excusable, but even more basic (indeed, very likely a major contributor to some of these failures) was the fact that the people of the United States had decided that the war was a hopeless, perhaps even immoral, cause. Selective service, the twelve-month rotation system, and the excellent mail and even telephone service that had buoyed the morale of pre-Tet soldiers now ensured that home-front disaffection steadily eroded the legitimacy of the entire chain of command charged with continuing the fight and passing the torch to the South Vietnamese in an orderly fashion.

This loss of legitimacy not only emasculated the army as an organization, but, as it has become apparent in the last decade, also caused lasting pain for an enormous number of young Americans who had survived their year in combat only to return to an unsympathetic, even hostile civilian world. Estimates of the number of Vietnam veterans suffering from posttraumatic stress disorder (PTSD) run as high as 1.5 million (2.8 million military served in Vietnam altogether).[32] While it is no doubt true that a certain percentage of veterans from all wars are plagued by dreams and nightmares related to their wartime experiences, the relative paucity of literature on postcombat reactions in World War II and Korean veterans seems to indicate that outward manifestations of discontent or maladjustment are far more common among Vietnam vets. This war certainly differed from its forerunners in a number of respects, and more and more PTSD researchers and clinicians are being brought to focus on the real differences in the homecoming experiences of the veterans of the three wars. The combination of rapid return of individual soldiers to the United States and civilian life with indifference, fear, or outright hostility on the part of the civilian populace apparently prevented many veterans from "working through" their experiences and achieving the sense of closure attained by the vast majority of older veterans, who came home on troopships to a supportive and often hero-worshipping public. Empirical surveys of both soldiers[33] and Veterans Administration (VA) mental health professionals[34] have repeatedly identified social support upon return from Vietnam as a critical factor in the development of PTSD, often more critical than the intensity of the combat experienced or the social support received while in Vietnam.[35] That is, PTSD symptoms were most prevalent and most intense among Vietnam vets who experienced negative reactions from friends, relatives, and society at large upon their return to the United States.

Lifton has asserted that the combat veteran of any war is faced with the task of attenuating indelible images of death and suffering and overcoming the anxiety and guilt that accompany them.[36] This task is greatly dependent upon finding meaning and justification for his fighting, killing, and even surviving. In past wars, the soldier has been aided immeasurably in this search by the assurances of family, friends, and community that his sacrifices are appreciated and are justified by the importance for all of them of what he has done. An article by Holm in fact emphasizes the apparent protection from PTSD provided many American Indian Vietnam vets by traditional tribal ceremonies purging warriors of the trauma of battle upon their return to their tribal community. Even without explicit ceremony, tribal traditions and customs often provide the resolution so often needed by veterans. A Cherokee veteran provides the following: "After I got home, my uncles sat me down and had me tell them what it was all about. One of them had been in the service in World War II and knew what war was like. We talked about what went on over there, about the killing and the waste and one of my uncles said that was why God's laws are against war. They never really talked about those kind of things with me before."[37]

As Holm points out, the important point here is that the veteran was able to share his experiences without being told, directly or indirectly, that his actions were improper. His participation in the war was seen simply as something that young men have to do, and, although his accounts of combat confirmed the Cherokee belief that war is the ultimate evil, his own bravery and service were cheered. The veteran himself was considered to have gained maturity and wisdom beyond his years.

Although the VA's exhaustive study *Legacies of Vietnam* mentions a similar ability of some small-town communities to distinguish between the war and its warriors, the great majority of Vietnam veterans found their community of little help. Indeed, as Fallows described it: "to those who opposed the war, the ones who served were, first, animals and killers; then 'suckers' who were trapped by the system, deserving pity but no respect; and finally, invisible men. . . . A returned veteran might win limited redemption if he publicly recanted. . . . Otherwise he was expected to keep his experiences to himself.[38]

Our confidence in this theory of PTSD etiology has been considerably increased by recent reports from Israeli Defence Force colleagues that approximately 40 percent of the combat stress reaction in the Lebanon campaign was "late reactions," soldiers who have satisfactorily completed their military duties and developed a PTSD-like combat stress reaction after apparently uneventful periods at home.[39] Just as America had a decade before, Israel saw public support for the continued occupation of Lebanon wane steadily as it became clear that this was not the typical Israeli surgical strike, but rather a Vietnam-like quagmire. Such late reactions were rarely if ever seen in 1973, when public support for the war was universal, despite the fact that overall stress reaction rates were 50 percent higher than in Lebanon.

CONCLUSIONS

It has been our intention in preparing this chapter to trace a gradual evolution in the sources of soldier motivation and commitment. The central issue is the psychological legitimation of killing. What is it that makes killing legitimate, even desirable, in some contexts and illegitimate in others? We have suggested that the past three millenia have seen a transition which has gradually disconnected three powerful sources of legitimacy for the soldier. In ancient times, and even today in "unsophisticated" societies, it was one's duty to society (and its gods) that impelled the soldier to risk his life in combat. However, the soldier of those times was also bound by his duty as a soldier and his duty to his immediate fighting partners. The rise of specialized and mercenary armies made the importance of the former of these (chivalric code and warrior ethic) more apparent, and the need for dispersal occasioned by twentieth-century weapons led to what may have been an overemphasis on the importance of small-group bonds. The evidence of Korea, Vietnam, and Lebanon suggests that this support is inadequate in the long run except in the context of a "latent ideology" involving at least an unspoken commitment to the soldier's social system, a feeling that his role as a soldier is important to its well-being, and confidence that his actions have some real consequences.[40]

What then of future wars? And what are the implications for the U.S. military? The U.S. Army if anything is more disconnected from and unrepresentative of American society than fifteen years ago, when conscription was abolished. Few college graduates enlist in today's armed forces, despite an increasing need for intelligent and resourceful soldiers to man and maintain sophisticated, expensive weapon systems and carry out an "airland battle" doctrine which relies heavily on initiative and flexibility down to the squad level. The army is more than 25 percent black now, and has a rapidly growing Spanish-speaking segment as well. Perhaps more serious than either educational or ethnic unrepresentativeness is the potential for problems in combat engendered by the nearly completely economic inducements to enlistment sustaining recruiting. Perhaps this is an unavoidable reflection of the attitudes of today's American youth toward military service, but it conjures up a vision of a Potemkin army ready, willing, and able to serve in peacetime, but without a solid foundation for combat. Initiatives like the army's Unit Manning System, which is gradually turning the combat arms from an individual-oriented into a unit-oriented organization by keeping soldiers together for the duration of their enlistment, is making significant headway in enhancing interpersonal bonds among small-unit members, and in a very short war this may be enough.

The active Army's current size guarantees that no matter what its level of commitment it can successfully deal with only low-intensity and the first phases of mid- to high-intensity conflict. Any prolonged trial of arms will require a rapid restructuring of the relationship between the mass of the American population and the military service. An imperative for the future then lies in the concepts of legitimacy of war and combat held by the population at large. Without a national consensus about "what we fight for," any decision to enter armed conflict is rife with possibilities for splitting the body politic and the military establishment as it was split in Vietnam. Our historical overview has illustrated that the bases of combat legitimacy change as cultures change. Ours is a rapidly changing culture, and a new consensus as to legitimacy may be reached. Such a consensus will emerge only as the product of a consensus about our goals as a nation and when a reasonable society may resort to armed conflict in defense of those goals. That consensus is not yet with us. The freedom and pluralism that sound so noble in the abstract have become a sort of "equal time" doctrine which makes no judgment, allows no preferences, and provides no guidance to its guardians.[41] We have no doubt our forces will answer the call from their commander-in-chief whenever it comes. We pray, for their sakes and ours, that if it comes soon they can accomplish their mission rapidly.[42]

NOTES

1. Thucydides, *History of the Peloponnesian War* (New York: Penguin, 1978), pp. 400–408.

2. William Shakespeare, *Henry V*, Act 4, Scene 2, in *The Works of William Shakespeare*, ed. W.G. Clark and W.A. Wright (New York: Doubleday, n.d.).

3. G. Dumezeil, *The Destiny of the Warrior* (Chicago: University of Chicago Press, 1970).

4. Walter Burkett, *Greek Religion* (Cambridge, Mass.: Harvard University Press, 1985).

5. Vegetius, "The Military Institution of the Romans," in *Roots of Strategy*, ed. T.R. Phillips (Harrisburg, Pa.: Stackpole Books, 1985).

6. P. Bondanella and M. Musa, eds., *The Portable Machiavelli* (New York: Viking, 1979).

7. Prabhavanandas and Isherwoods, trans., *The Song of God: Bhagavad-Gita* (New York: Mentor, 1972).

8. W. Kendrick Pritchett, *The Greek State at War*, Part II (Berkeley: University of California Press, 1974).

9. Bondanella and Musa, *The Portable Machiavelli*.

10. Barbara W. Tuchman, *A Distant Mirror* (New York: Ballantine, 1978).

11. J.R. Hale, *War and Society in Renaissance Europe* (Baltimore: Johns Hopkins University Press, 1985), pp. 1450–1620.

12. L. White, *The Virgin and the Dynamo* (Berkeley: University of California Press, 1950).

13. Tuchman, *A Distant Mirror*.

14. Alfred Vagts, *A History of Militarism, Civilian and Military* (New York: The Free Press, 1967), pp. 72–73.

15. Quoted in John C. Baynes, *Morale* (New York: Praeger, 1967), p. 182.

16. H. Gerth and C.W. Mills, eds., *From Max Weber: Essays in Sociology* (New York: Oxford Press, 1958).

17. Vegetius, "The Military Institution of the Romans."

18. Ibid.

19. Ardant DuPicq, *Battle Studies: Ancient and Modern*, trans. J.N. Greeley and R.C. Cotton (Harrisburg, Pa.: Military Service Publishing, 1958).

20. Samuel Stouffer et al., *The American Soldier* (Princeton, N.J.: Princeton University Press, 1949).

21. Edward Shils and Morris Janowitz, "Cohesion and Disintegration in the Wehrmacht in World War II," *Public Opinion Quarterly* 12 (1948), pp. 280–315.

22. W.S. Mullins and Albert J. Glass, *Neuropsychiatry in World War II*, Volume II: *Overseas Theaters* (Washington, D.C.: Office of the Surgeon General, Department of the Army, 1973).

23. Stouffer et al., *The American Soldier*.

24. Tony Ashworth, *Trench Warfare, 1914–1918: The Live and Let Live System* (New York: Holmes and Meier, 1980), pp. 207–10.

25. Baynes, *Morale*, p. 99.

26. Ashworth, *Trench Warfare*, pp. 216–17.

27. S.L.A. Marshall, *Men against Fire* (New York: William Morrow, 1947).

28. Roger Little, "Buddy Relations and Combat Performance," in *The New Military*, ed. Morris Janowitz (New York: Russell Sage Foundation, 1964), pp. 195–224.

29. Faris R. Kirkland, "The French Military Collapse in 1940: A Psychohistorical Interpretation," *The Journal of Psychohistory* 12 (1985), pp. 313–37.

30. John J. Marren, "Psychiatric Problems in Troops in Korea during and Following Combat," *U.S. Armed Forces Medical Journal* 75, pp. 715–26.

31. Richard Gabriel and Paul Savage, *Crisis in Command* (New York: Hill and Wang, 1978).

32. L. Harris & Associates, *Myths and Realities: A Study of Attitudes toward Vietnam Veterans*, U.S. Senate Committee on Veterans Affairs, Print No. 29 (Washington, D.C.: U.S. Government Printing Office, 1980).

33. J. Frye and R. Stockton, "Discriminant Analysis of Post-Traumatic

Stress Disorder among a Group of Vietnam Veterans," *American Journal of Psychiatry* 139 (1982), pp. 52–56.

34. T. Keane and J. Fairbank, "Survey Analysis of Combat Related Stress Disorders in Vietnam Veterans," *American Journal of Psychiatry* 140 (1983), pp. 48–50.

35. Robert A. Stretch, "Post-Traumatic Stress Disorders among Vietnam and Vietnam-Era Veterans," in *Trauma and Its Wake: The Study and Treatment of Post-Traumatic Stress Disorder*, ed. Charles R. Figley (New York: Brunner-Mazel, 1985).

36. Robert Lifton, "Death Imprints on Youth in Vietnam," *Journal of Clinical Child Psychology* 3 (1974), pp. 47–49.

37. Tom Holm, "Culture, Ceremonialism, and Stress: American Indian Veterans and the Vietnam War," *Armed Forces and Society* 12 (1986), pp. 237–51.

38. James Fallows, quoted by James Webb, "Vietnam Vets Didn't Kill Babies and They Aren't Suicidal," *Washington Post*, April 6, 1986, p. cl.

39. Zahava Solomon, "A 3–year Prospective Study of Post-Traumatic Stress Disorder in Israeli Combat Veterans," *Journal of Traumatic Stress* 2 (1989), pp. 59–73.

40. Charles C. Moskos, *The American Enlisted Man* (New York: Russell Sage Foundation, 1970).

41. D.A. Zoll, "A Crisis in Self-Image: The Role of the Military in American Culture," *Parameters* 12, no. 4 (1982), pp. 24–31.

42. The views of the authors do not purport to reflect the position of the Department of the Army or the Department of Defense (Para 4–3, AR 360–5).

6

State and Conscience: Stages of Conscientious Objection to Military Service

Charles C. Moskos

If the citizen-soldier can be traced back to the origins of the modern Western state, an almost equally durable social type is the conscientious objector. Although a long-standing phenomenon, only in recent years has conscientious objection become a major factor affecting armed forces and society. Indeed, any accounting of the sociology of the military and international security in the advanced industrialized states must take into account pacifism in general, and conscientious objection in particular.

Conscientious objection as we know it first took shape in America, chiefly in Pennsylvania and New England, where religious pacifists in the seventeenth century won the right to refuse to bear arms. This right was reaffirmed by the Lincoln administration on an ad hoc basis in the American Civil War. During the two world wars of the twentieth century, conscientious objection grew in the United States and also took root in Great Britain and its English-speaking dominions. In the 1950s, conscientious objection became a recognized right in Scandinavia, the Low Countries, and the Federal Republic of Germany. Indeed, on the contemporary scene, conscientious objection has been given more latitude in the Federal Republic of Germany than in any other country. By the 1970s, some very

limited conscientious objection was allowed in the NATO countries of Mediterranean Europe. During the 1980s, conscientious
objectors appeared in the socialist countries of Eastern Europe
and in such diverse countries as South Africa, Switzerland, Sin-
gapore, and Israel. In brief, with only a few exceptions, man-
datory military service in the contemporary era is accompanied
by forms of conscientious objection.

Even more striking is the fact that conscientious objection now
occurs even among service members whose conscience changed
while on military duty, including those who initially volunteered
for military service. Another variant of conscientious objection
is directed itself toward particular types of warfare, notably nuclear weapons—a form of objection that has appeared both in
and out of the armed forces. To date, however, no country has
yet allowed "selective" conscientious objection, that is exemption from military service on the basis of objection to a particular
war or category of war.

Although much has been written about conscientious objection (albeit on a limited range of countries), almost all of this
writing is philo-pacifist.[1] Conceptual generalization is virtually
nil. Among social science writings, the literature is sparse and
limited to analyses of the incidence of conscientious objection,
public opinion survey data, and trends in legal definitions of
conscience.[2] Again, conceptual generalization operates at a low
level, at best.

This chapter places conscientious objection in a conceptual
context, one that relates the dimensions of conscientious objection to each other. The main dimensions are seen as the state
criteria of conscience, the patterns of objection, and the state
policy toward conscientious objection. What follows, then, is
the first effort to examine conscientious objection within a broad
sociological framework.

The main thesis is that, even taking into account national
singularities and varying social histories, a remarkably consistent
pattern characterizes the social evolution of conscientious objection, especially in Western parliamentary democracies. One
can even talk of fairly distinct and sequential stages that characterize the relation between the state and conscientious objec-

tion. These stages roughly correspond to societies that are preindustrial, early industrial, late industrial, and postindustrial.

The protostage, characteristic of seventeenth- and eighteenth-century Western societies, finds conscientious objectors existing in a limbo world where the state, variously and inconsistently, permits unofficial objection, allows purchase of exemption, or metes out severe punishment. The conscientious objectors in this stage are almost always life-long members of traditional "peace" churches, notably the Quakers emerging out of an English tradition and Mennonites and Church of the Brethren coming out of a German pietistic and Anabaptist tradition. By the mid-nineteenth century, the traditional peace sects were joined by the newer Seventh Day Adventists and later the Jehovah Witnesses. Early on, the sociology of the conscientious objectors was diverse. Quakers generally represented a well-educated urban element; the much more numerous Mennonites and Brethren were rural based. The Adventists and Witnesses brought in an urban proletarian element. In common to all these groups, however, was a refusal to bear arms.

The three dimensions of state criteria of conscientious objection, the patterns of conscientious objection, and the state policy toward conscientious objection—serve as a unifying framework for the stages of conscientious objection, as indicated in Table 6.1.

In stage I, the state formally recognizes conscientious objection but limits such recognition to the traditional peace churches. In stage II, any religiously based objection is accepted by the state; conscience status is now granted to objectors coming from mainline Protestant bodies and, later, Roman Catholics, as well as traditional pacifists. In the United States, Black Muslims became visible conscientious objectors during World War II, as did American Jews during the Vietnam War. Stage III sees the crossing of a major boundary: the definition of conscience vastly expands to include secular and philosophical motives. In effect, religion is no longer a determining factor.

The state policy toward conscientious objection parallels the state's changing definition of conscience. In stage I, the state allows conscientious objectors to serve in a noncombat capacity

Table 6.1
State and Conscience

	State Criteria of Conscientious Objection	State Policy Toward Conscientious Objection	Patterns of Conscientious Objection
Proto-Stage	conscientious objectors exist in a limbo world where the state, variously and inconsistently, permits unofficial exemption, allows purchase of exemption, or metes out severe punishment		
Stage I	life-long membership in traditional "peace" church	non-combatant military duty	avoidance of military service for all religious COs
Stage II	above plus any religion-based objection to military service	alternative civil service under military aegis (perhaps church interface)	avoidance of military service for all COs
Stage III	above plus secular philosophy based objection to military service	alternative civil service under civilian aegis	general opposition to military system; special opposition to time differential between military and civil service

within the armed services. Stage II sees the appearance of alternative civil service under some form of military aegis (such as the conscription system). This pattern may also see church bodies playing an intermediary role between the state and the alternative servers. Stage III sees a movement toward complete civilian service, a trend that diminishes the role of the intervening church bodies.

The conscientious objectors themselves undergo parallel changes in their relations to the state. In stage I, the leadership of the conscientious objection movement is largely in the hands of the traditional peace churches, who, however, scrupulously advocate an exemption for all religious conscientious objectors (COs). By stage II, the leadership expands to include some from the mainline churches (which remain internally divided on conscientious objection). The modal pattern is to push for blanket CO exemptions from military service. In stage III, the CO establishment, which now includes secularists, moves toward a general opposition to the military system, with special emphasis on doing away with any time differential between military and civilian service. Thus, limited engagement with the polity gives way to political (and perhaps extraparliamentary) confrontations with the state military system.

There is another line of reasoning to consider. It appears that conscientious objectors will increasingly define their alternative service in civic, even perhaps political, rather than religious terms. Will willingness to perform alternative civil service become the standard of conscientious objection (as it has already, de facto, in West Germany)? Will prior membership in an antimilitary group become the functional equivalent of membership in a traditional peace church? That is, as earlier judgments of conscientious objection took into account sectarian membership, future definitions may take into account participation in antiwar or antimilitary activities.

No scheme of broad societal change can be as neat and tidy as the stages of conscientious objection presented here.[3] In particular, differences in the timing (though not sequence) of the stages may occur between parliamentary Western societies and socialist Eastern European states. Yet, the historical and crossnational data seem to fit the paradigm remarkably well. The sum effect of these trends is a secularization of conscientious objection.

NOTES

1. See, for example, Peter Brock, *Twentieth-Century Pacifism* (New York: Van Nostrand Reinhold, 1970); Lawrence S. Wittner, *Rebels against War* (Philadelphia: Temple University Press, 1984); Stephen M. Kohn, *Jailed for Peace* (Westport, Conn.: Greenwood Press, 1986); and Caroline Moorehead, *Troublesome People* (London: Hamish Hamilton, 1987).

2. See Hugh Smith, "Conscientious Objection in Australia," Ruth Meyer and Hans Jorg Schweizer, "Conscientious Objection in Switzerland," and Mauritz S. Mortenson, "Conscientious Objection in Norway," in papers presented at the XI World Congress of Sociology, New Delhi, India, August 1986, published in *Forum International 5* (Munich, West Germany: SOWI, 1987), pp. 243–332.

3. Conscientious objection arising out of a non-Christian (or non-Jewish) tradition would make a fascinating study.

7

The Threat to the Legitimacy of War Posed by the Fallen Soldier: The Case of Israel

Eugene C. Weiner

The inevitable fact that soldiers are killed is not an issue about which a nation at war can remain indifferent, that is if it wants the civilian population to support the war and wants soldiers to fight in it.

Families who are bitter and accusatory toward the military must be considered by any military establishment that wishes to continue to fulfill its functions. Such a family published the following vengeful lament after the death of their son in the Lebanon War:

Raviv, to your fresh green grave I have come.
In the name of all those responsible for the event
I have come to ask forgiveness.
I ask your forgiveness for the Defense Minister
who made the hasty decision to storm unoccupied Beirut.
I ask your forgiveness for the Division Commander
that threw your Nahal brigade into battle precipitously.
I ask your forgiveness in the name of your battalion
commander
Who sent two young tank commanders out on a singular
and difficult mission,
I ask your forgiveness in the name of the Brigade
commander of the Nahal who conducted the battle

in an incompetent manner.
I ask your forgiveness in the name of Zev the tank
commander who fled from the battle and abandoned a
friend in dire straits.
I ask your forgiveness for the Captain who was to
bring reinforcements, who didn't trouble himself or
endanger himself to provide the support you needed.
I ask your forgiveness for all those Nahal officers
in the rear lines who didn't extend themselves
to evacuate the wounded from the cave.
I ask forgiveness, as it is written in the liturgy
on the Holy Days of Awe:
"And for all these Sins, Forgive us, Forgive us,
Have compassion upon us, and Exonerate us."

                                              Author Unknown

If the military, as an institution, wishes to maintain its legitimacy in the estimation of military personnel and civilians alike,
it *must* address the devastating sense of loss felt by the relatives
and friends of fallen soldiers. Somehow it must allocate the
resources and have the procedures to deal with the need to
explain the deaths of loved ones in an understandable and acceptable manner. Even that is not enough. Such deaths must be
officially acknowledged and commemorated. Such deaths must
be placed within rational and publicly recognized frameworks;
these deaths must be legitimated.

The legitimacy of death in wars comes from a belief that somehow the bases for hostilities are fundamentally correct: The war
is being fought for a morally justifiable cause; it is being pursued
by those who are authorized to lead the nation in arms; and
these leaders are conducting the war with some degree of competence. It is these beliefs that help justify the personal sacrifice
necessary in armed struggles. For most people, however, these
beliefs are just abstractions. When tragedy hits home and a loved
one is killed in war, the psychic cost of maintaining these abstract
beliefs becomes painfully real. In many cases, the belief in the
legitimacy of sacrifice of life is severely challenged and found
wanting, resulting in second thoughts which can deeply affect
the conduct of war.

When thoughts about the worthwhileness of sacrifice remain

within the private realm of limited circles of bereaved relatives and friends, there is no immediate threat to the overall public legitimacy of war; however, when such reservations run rampant and become public issues, the very purposes that impel nations to fight and to maintain armies are called into question. When this happens, particular wars and the military institutions that support them are in great danger of losing legitimacy.

The crisis of legitimacy may be concretely expressed in a variety of ways. It could be through a loss of morale among the fighting troops, through an unwillingness of the public at large to allocate resources toward the pursuit of hostilities, or both. The strength of these factors can cause armies to cease functioning as effective fighting units. In all armies and societies the poorly explained, incompetently commemorated death of soldiers is a potential catalyst for a crisis of legitimacy.

SOME SPECIAL CHARACTERISTICS OF THE ISRAELI SITUATION

This chapter deals briefly with the attempts of one nation, Israel, to handle this difficult issue of fallen soldiers. In doing this, we must point out that, although many of the specific issues dealt with by the Israeli military are representative of other nations and other armies, not all are.

In Israel certain factors have coalesced to make the military's handling of bereavement particularly important. Most families in Israel have been traumatized by memories of the Holocaust either directly or indirectly. For those families who had members in concentration camps during World War II, the strength of the Israeli Army is a necessary compensation for the feelings of helplessness and impotence that were the lot of camp victims. Losing a relative or a friend in war calls that strength into question, and one frequently experiences a return of that hopelessness and impotent rage that characterized the camp victim. The 250,000 former inmates of such camps who live in Israel are particularly mindful of the horrors of death. For them the loss of a loved one frequently triggers a whole world of horrible associations that are barely under control in the best of circumstances. Their feelings for their children are not only those usual and widespread ones; they are tinged with the feeling that these children are surrogates for those relatives who died in horror in World War II. Living children in Israel bear the heavy emotional burden of being surrogates for millions of their dead uncles, aunts, and grandparents who perished at the hands of the Nazis. When these children themselves are killed, the anguish and bitterness of surviving parents and relatives are overwhelming. For those in the society with no direct experience of the Holocaust, its relative recency creates an aura of tragedy which pervades the entire society and reinforces the bereaved individual's sense of loss.

In addition, the incessant wars since 1948 have created a permanent condition of exposure to death in battle. Some 12,000 individuals have died in war in Israel since the state came into being. In the period from 1947 to 1949, 4,558 soldiers and 1,100 civilians were killed; during the border skirmishes and campaigns of retribution, 1,138; the Sinai Campaign, 176; duty in the border patrol and the military police, 759; the Six Day War, 789; the War of Attrition, 669; the Yom Kippur War, 2,686; and the Lebanon War, over 700. Some 18,000 families in Israel are bereaved, including nearly 3,500 war widows. The fact that Israel has a citizen army means that virtually every household in Israel has some member who is exposed to the dangers of war. The average male in Israel does about seven years of active military service between the ages of 18 and 54, not infrequently in combat circumstances. Everyone in Israel is exposed to the constant threat of terrorist attack. The large numbers of terrorist attacks, bombings, and killings mean that the issue of bereavement is always potentially on the agenda of families and of the society at large. Death caused by hostilities is ubiquitous in Israel. It has been that way ever since 1929.

The relatively small size of the population and the particularly closely knit nature of the society create conditions where it is virtually certain that large numbers of people will know those who have been killed in hostilities and will experience the resulting resentment, panic, and despair, which could reach contagious proportions. When I asked a random group of Israelis how many of them had lost an immediate relative or a very close childhood friend in the hostilities, 70 percent above the age of

18 replied they had been so bereaved. By comparison it was not uncommon during the Vietnam hostilities for whole segments of the American public to have had no contact with bereaved families, in spite of the fact that more than 50,000 American soldiers were killed. Indeed, many Americans had no friends or relatives who even served in the army, let alone suffered casualties in the war. This is inconceivable in Israel.

The lack of geographical distance in Israel between the front lines, where until the present most of the fighting has taken place, and the population centers creates great personal involvement between what happens on the battle lines and what happens at home. Death is not isolated geographically—it is not something that happens in some remote "over there." In Israel war is very much in the "here and now." This geographical proximity also influences the way in which bereavement on the home front impacts the soldiers in battle. The contagion effects are potentially reciprocal due to the high degree of communication between the home front and the battle front. It is not uncommon for families to have "representatives" on every front who keep them informed about their loved ones. In future wars, it is not unlikely that fighting units will have their own representatives on the home front, particularly if that home front is going to be subject to bombardment, which seems likely. At present the home front's representatives on the fighting front are frequently friends, relatives, and neighbors. On occasion there are informal and militarily illegal forays of civilians who go to the front looking for their missing relatives.

There is no significant geographical distance between the front and the home. Consequently, hardly any time at all lapses between the time a disaster occurs and the time it becomes common knowledge. Informal networks of communication among Israelis see to that. Consequently, the Israeli military has had to develop a fast and accurate system to keep its citizens informed about losses in battle. If the military does not act quickly, it is highly likely that the informal means of communication in Israel's tightly knit society will preempt the military communication channels which were set up to deal with the issue of notification of loss of life. There is a greater chance of an inaccurate report reaching the family through informal communication channels.

When the army does not present the circumstances surrounding the death first, the credibility of its explanation is significantly lowered. The army authorities in Israel do everything in their power to be the first to get to the family with the bad news. The authorities in the Israeli military are well aware, as was William Shakespeare, that "the first bringer of unwelcome news hath but a losing office, and his tongue sounds ever after as a sullen bell"; nonetheless, it would sound more sullen still if it did not fulfill its responsibility as the first conveyer of the news, bad as it is.

The deeply humanistic value placed on individual life in Israeli society makes the loss of the single soldier a major event not only for the family involved but for the society at large. Golda Meir reportedly issued instructions to her military aide during her term as prime minister that she was to be awakened from her sleep whenever an Israeli soldier was killed in combat in the period prior to the Yom Kippur War. The death of every soldier diminishes everyone in peculiarly intense ways. In addition to the importance of the living person, there is a particularly intense set of feelings about the fear of being demographically diminished whenever a soldier is killed. Jews feel themselves to be a struggling minority. One-third of the Jewish people was destroyed in World War II, and the Jews of Israel are outnumbered by the surrounding Arab population more than thirty times over. So, aside from the significance of the human life in Israeli society, there is a particularly intense sense of anxiety about a shrinking population. The high incidence of death and maiming in Israeli society as a result of hostilities during the past thirty-eight years has made bereavement a matter of the utmost importance to the military establishment not only because of concern for human values but also for its potentially disruptive political and military effects.

These potentially disruptive effects became actualized and the issue of bereavement helped to energize a mass political protest movement following the Yom Kippur War in 1973–1974, which resulted in the fall of the Labor government after twenty-six years of power. Moshe Dayan, the defense minister at the time, was regarded by the public at large as the person responsible for Israel's being caught unprepared for Egypt's surprise attack which resulted in a heavy loss of life. He could hardly appear in public without being angrily accosted by scores of bereaved parents of fallen soldiers.

The Israeli attitude to fallen soldiers is much influenced by the Jewish religious and cultural traditions concerning bereavement. The tradition creates a climate within which the military institutions have to exist, and military procedures have to respect and reflect the values of this tradition.

The Jewish tradition is realistic, ritualistic, and constructionist in regard to death and bereavement. It is realistic in its assessment of the profound depths of human emotions that are associated with loss. It makes no attempt to inhibit the full expression of the highly personal and individualized emotions that are evoked by bereavement. In fact, the tradition allows the bereaved free rein within rather broadly defined limits. Bereaved persons are given license to express all the pain and anguish associated with the bereaved condition in whichever way they wish. There are few if any sanctions against giving in to one's emotions at a time of bereavement. It is expected behavior.

The codified norms of the Jewish legal tradition cautions that a person seeking to comfort a mourner should not ask how the person feels. It is an idle question. There is no way for the mourner to describe the feeling of loss unless they spontaneously choose to do so. Visitors to the home of mourners are encouraged to speak only if the mourner wishes to speak. In the face of death, the most eloquent comment is sometimes silence itself. If the mourner wishes to laugh, the visitor is encouraged to join if possible; if the mourner wishes to speak, the visitor is encouraged to follow the lead and speak. It is assumed that mourning is a very individual affair and that each person mourns in his or her own way. It is the task of those who wish to offer comfort to do so in a way that is responsive to the flow of emotions from the mourner. Since these emotions are unpredictable, the visitor is to take his or her lead from the mourner. Emotional expression is the expected behavior, but the form that expression takes is individual.

The Jewish tradition is ritualistic in that there are prescribed behaviors associated with the passage of time. It is assumed that mourning is a process which requires time to run its psychological course. The time boundaries of the "working through" process are delineated ritualistically. They are marked by ceremonials that are carefully stipulated within four defined time frames. First, there are rules that guide behavior in the period before the burial. A second set of rules guides the behavior after the burial until the conclusion of the seven days of mourning during which time the mourner stays at home and is available to the friends and relatives of the deceased. The third set of rules relates to behavior until the end of thirty days after the death of the deceased. The fourth set relates to behavior until the conclusion of the first eleven months.

The Jewish tradition is constructionist in its use of the mourning period to achieve prescribed social goals. Mourning is an occasion for the strengthening of family group ties and for the numerous gatherings of networks of the friends, relatives, and groups of which the deceased was a part. It is an occasion for the giving of funds to institutions and worthy causes that the deceased supported. These secondary gains of the mourning situation are important in terms of strengthening the group. Families are reunited in their moment of sorrow. Groups are strengthened because the members have to reassess the group aims in light of the void created by the death of one of its members. In material terms the institutions of society are strengthened by the contributions given in the name of the deceased. The secondary gains of mourning and bereavement are intrinsically constructionist. They are intended to reinforce and support the structures of society.

The military in Israel has wisely decided to take cognizance of these religious and cultural traditions and to adapt itself accordingly. The services it renders to families are themselves realistic, ritualized, and constructionist. A woman who is notified that her husband has been killed needs someone to look after her children until she can begin to function properly—the army will pay for a babysitter. She may need someone to help her notify her children that their father has been killed. The same person who notified her will frequently stay and help her tell her children. The services are ritualized and vary within different time frames. The memorial department does not immediately appear on the scene to help the mourning family collect the literary memorabilia to publish a memorial book—it appears on the scene when the time is ripe. The social worker who provides information about financial help, which the Defense Department extends to the bereaved, also appears at the appropriate time. Finally, it is constructionist in that it tries to make the best of what is a tragedy for the family. It tries to organize peer support groups from other similarly stricken by tragedy. Within the bounds of good taste, the military attempts to celebrate the heroism and moral virtues of the fallen soldier in order to strengthen the society's resolve and morale.

Rabbis are involved from the very beginning of the process of dealing with the death of soldiers. Those that search the battlefield for the dead are men associated with the *Chevra Kadisha*, "the Holy Society." They are engaged in caring for the body once it is located. They, together with other army authorities, are involved in the identification procedures. The chief rabbi of the Israeli Army has a helicopter at his disposal and oversees a large staff of field rabbis who are with troops in combat. When a soldier has been killed in battle, they help prepare the body for transport to a regional army hospital. Once the body is released by the medical authorities, the rabbis are responsible for all subsequent procedures. They cooperate in doing all that is possible to prevent families from seeing the remains of their family members. The sight of the demolished body of a dear one can leave scars for the survivors' lifetimes.

The religious authorities of the military in Israel are involved in the preburial rituals such as purification and preparation of the body for burial. Together with the regional army officer, known in Israel as the "officer of the city" (*Katzin Ha-ir*), they are responsible for the burial and mourning rituals. They bring the body to the cemetary, prepare the grave, and help the family arrange their home for the mourning ritual. The religious functionaries have a say in the organization of the house of mourning. They are available for consultation and for support, and they maintain continuous contact with the family not only during the eleven months of mourning, but also for the yearly anniversary of the death of the soldier and during the special commemorative days for years to come after the tragedy. One can say that there is a very close relationship in Israel between the military and the religious authorities, a relationship that is rarely challenged even by the most secular of Israel's Jews. For the non-Jewish groups in Israel who are involved in the military, such as the Druze and the Beduin, virtually all arrangements for burial and mourning are conducted by the religious authorities of their communities.

MILITARY PRACTICE: HUMANE TREATMENT AND COOLING PEOPLE OUT

Bereavement practices in the Israeli military are much influenced by the nature of the organization of which they are a part. The ways in which the army institutionalizes its procedures are typical of hierarchical, bureaucratic military organizations. Military regulations guiding the behavior of personnel are as predetermined as circumstances allow. As little as is possible is left to chance. When departures from predetermined patterns do occur they are often occasions of stress and tension for those who are performing the functions. Every effort is made to foresee all possible contingencies and to learn from past mistakes. In dealing with the issue of fallen soldiers, the army is dealing with a situation in extremis where the smallest mistake or impropriety is remembered for a long time, and military personnel can be made to pay a high price through the official censure of superiors. When it comes to the burial of a young soldier, emotions are raw. The situation by its very nature is emotionally volcanic. Bitterness and anger are almost always on the verge of bursting the bounds of restraint.

In order to handle the danger of the violent outburst of emotions, the military institutions have had to devote resources to "cool out," using Erving Goffman's phrase, those individuals who have suffered the most grievous loss that wars impose; that is, the loss of a spouse, parent, child, brother, or other relative, or a friend. In pointing this out I do not mean to infer that the Israeli military inherently lacks compassion for the sufferings of the bereaved. From my own work with the psychological division of the Israeli Army I have observed that the opposite is most frequently the case. But I wish to make the claim that bereavement which is occasioned by the death of combatants is a problem for the military as an institution. If the military does not deal with bereavement successfully, the resentment generated by unrestrained grief could have widespread political effects in a free and democratic society and prevent the military institution from doing what they are designed to do: to make war. In the end, armies depend on allegiance and assent which are vulnerable and open to influence by contagious emotions. Few human emotions are as intense or as volatile as those connected with death and mourning, and so, in order for the army to be able to continue fighting, it is necessary to help the bereaved deal with their feelings about their fallen loved ones.

How does an army actually achieve this? In Israel, the army and the adjunct offices of the defense department have assumed responsibility for the following tasks in regard to the issue of fallen soldiers:

1. Identification of the deceased
2. Care for the body until burial
3. Notification of the immediate family
4. Caring for the physical and psychological well-being of those being notified
5. Making arrangements for the funeral
6. Planning and performing the ceremony at the grave site
7. Helping the family with the necessary ritual articles for the house of mourning
8. Administration of miscellaneous services which the defense department and the army accords to families

In addition to these direct care services there are others which deal with ceremonial aspects designed to perpetuate the memory of the fallen soldiers. These include the organization of days of remembrance, the construction and consecration of suitable war memorials, the publication of books of remembrance, and other kinds of memorial activities. One has here, in a brief, by no means exhaustive, summary, what is, in actuality, a vast corpus of regulations and procedures that are implemented by thousands of army and civilian personnel in a sizeable bureaucratic structure.

When the system works, it works very well. When it does not work, all hell breaks loose. One then sees the awesome potential of death in the military to create havoc. Outrage over the mishandling of the issue of fallen soldiers mobilizes vast public energies. The overall impact is analogous to a failed theodicy in the history of a religion. When God fails, religion goes through a crisis because there is no convincing explanation of how the God of the group can allow defeat and tragedy to happen to the pious faithful. Civilizations, societies, and religions are destroyed when theodicies chronically fail to provide satisfactory explanations for disaster. When they do their work, the greatest of disasters fail to lower the group morale.

The best example of this situation is the way in which theodicy succeeded among the Jews after the destruction of the Second Temple in the year 70 C.E. Disaster and destruction were all around, but the explanation that kept the people going was that they were being punished for their sins. It was not because their God had deserted them, but rather that they had sinned in the eyes of God. Armies are in the business of keeping the people "cooled out" around the issue of fallen soldiers.

SOME CASE STUDIES

The following brief synopses, in the form of case histories, are presented to illustrate how the system does or does not work in order to concretize the points previously considered.

Case Study One: When the System Works Well

Zev was killed in a tank during the Lebanon War. His body was found intact; his identification tags were where they should have been. The destruction of his tank was witnessed by other soldiers. His body was brought to the hospital in the northern part of Israel where it was identified. The details of his death were reported to the proper army authorities, and they gave the authorization to notify Zev's parents. The notification team was headed by a high army officer, a person known for his compassion and his ability to speak to people. The other members of the notification team were a physician and a psychologist. They had been on standby orders for just this kind of an assignment for two weeks, and they had had to notify the army at all times where they were. They went to the parents in uniform, found the address easily, and managed to gain entry into the apartment house without arousing the neighbors who knew what kind of news three army officers bring to families when they come to a neighborhood. The men notified the parents who were home at the time. No one needed medication. They stayed with the family for two hours until other family members had arrived from other parts of the city. The funeral took place the next morning at which time representatives from the son's unit constituted an honor guard. The family observed the seven days of mourning toward the end of which Zev's battalion commander came to the house to explain to the family just why the battle in which Zev died was important and the particular circumstances in which he was killed. The family collected all the letters that Zev had written to them from the army as well as those he had written to his girlfriend Zahava. A few friends who had been in school with Zev contributed essays about Zev, and, with the help of the defense department, they published a memorial book in his honor. Each Remembrance Day the parents together with Zahava and Zev's friends visit his grave. The defense department has been helping Zev's parents in various ways financially and psychologically over the years to help them bear their burden.

Case Study Two: The Wrong One Is Notified

"Yoram" was killed when he participated in a defensive action. He was killed in an army unit to which he had just been assigned at the very moment of mobilization. No one in the unit had met him before he became part of it. Proper identification of the body was made through tags found on the body. When the notification team came to the house to tell the family that Yoram had been killed, the mother shouted out that Yoram was not dead; on the contrary, he was at home and in the shower. The notification team head waited for Yoram to finish his shower and then asked him how his tags had come to be found on the body of a dead soldier. What emerged was that Yoram's brother Baruch had been called up to the army and had taken Yoram's identification tags. It was Baruch who had been killed. (Variations of this episode, which is an actual event, have happened in all of Israel's wars. Unlike this story, some have happier endings.)

Case Study Three: The Suicidal Father

Tzvi had been a part of a particularly elite unit that was involved in a mission which could not be discussed publicly. He had volunteered for the unit and the mission because there was a tradition of military bravery in the family. Both his father, who had been in a concentration camp, and his two brothers had distinguished themselves in various wars. The officer of the city—the *Katzin Ha-ir*, knew that the father was a little unbalanced mentally because of his own army and concentration camp experiences. He sent along a psychiatrist with the notification team because he expected trouble. When the family was notified that the son had been killed, the father made a lunge for the window of the apartment which was on the seventh floor. He was restrained, and army personnel stayed with him for a number of days until he had gotten over the initial stages of his remorse. Two months later, he was found dead on his son's grave. He had shot himself.

Case Study Four: Whose Negligence?

Five years ago Yochanan, who served in an army unit, decided to light the boiler to heat the water that his army unit needed. The boiler exploded. Someone had placed gasoline in the boiler instead of kerosene. He was burned to death. The army came to notify the family of the accident. After a thorough investigation of all those in the unit, it was still not clear who had placed the gasoline in the boiler. It could have been Yochanan himself. The father thought that this was impossible. Since that date, in spite of all the army could do to restrain him, the father has been engaged virtually full-time in speaking to all the members of the son's unit in order to ascertain the truth. This has gone on since the incident.

Case Study Five: Perpetual Mourning and Memorializing

Yossi was killed on the Suez Canal during the War of Attrition fifteen years ago. Since that time Yossi's family has devoted itself to finding appropriate memorials for him. They are convinced that his life was exemplary and that if all of Israel's youth knew about his life Israel would be a healthier society. To date, they have sponsored a yearly conference for educators about Israel's values which about 100 teachers attend; they have dedicated six Torah scrolls with his name on them in various synagogues; they have convinced the minister of the interior to dedicate a small forest in his honor; they have published four books of remembrances and essays that he wrote in school; they invite all the members of Yossi's graduating class as well as those in his army unit to their house every year on the anniversary of his death; they convinced their daughter to name her son Yossi; they frequently talk about what Yossi would be doing now were he alive; they go to all the memorial meetings of the organization for bereaved parents, the *Yad Labanim*; they are currently trying to convince the principal of the high school where Yossi studied to put his picture up on the remembrance wall; and they are in constant touch with the defense department authorities about new ways to perpetuate their son's memory.

Case Study Six: The Hero Who Was a Despicable Husband

Baruch died a hero's death. He defended his position for two days against an overwhelming force of enemy tanks and infantry. His bravery has become legendary. He was awarded posthumously the highest military honors that the State of Israel could give. His exploits are known by every schoolchild in Israel. When the army notified his wife that he had been killed she had a nervous breakdown. It took two years of therapy, paid for by the Defense Department, to uncover the pathological relationship that she had had with her husband. Her marriage was a living hell for her. Her joy that she was free of her husband now that he was dead was mixed with enormous feelings of guilt for having hated him. She not only has had to bear the burden of her own feelings of dislike for him, but she has had to be the symbol of the mourning, adoring wife who cherishes his memory. This is more than she could bear. The defense department organized a special group of war widows in which she can discuss, together with a clinical psychologist, her own ambivalent feelings in an environment that is not judgmental or threatening.

Many possible conclusions can be drawn from these case studies based on actual situations encountered in the Israeli military. The cases seem to illustrate the common ways in which people respond to tragic human events. We all know people who are destroyed by tragedy, who make mistakes, who build their lives on memories, who find it difficult to face their true feelings. The point of these case studies is that, for a military organization to function both in a humane way and in a manner that protects its own interests, it must deal with all these responses. This is especially true if the army is a citizen army, based largely on periodically mobilized civilians. There is no way that the Israeli military can ignore these all too human responses to tragedy and still remain what it is, an effective fighting force of mobilized civilians. There is no way the Israeli military can overlook the suicidal father, the family searching for the negligent perpetrator of their son's death, the perpetual mourner, the zealous searcher for perpetual memorialization, or the tortured wife of the national hero.

The Israeli military cannot overlook them for a number of reasons. First, they and their families are yesterday's, today's and tomorrow's soldiers. Without their active support, no one would be willing to serve in the army. Every soldier serving in the army looks at the way in which the army treats these people. Should something tragic happen to the soldier, these people could be his parents, wife, or child. Also, these bereaved people have a moral halo. They have a moral credit in the eyes of the society at large, for they have suffered so that the rest of the society could persist. Although every hero is a bore at last, as

Ralph Waldo Emerson has claimed, it is not the case with bereaved parents. They continue to maintain their special status in the society. They have had their nearest and dearest taken from them so that society could survive. As long as it does survive, society must express its compassion and gratitude. For a society to denigrate the sacrifices made in its name is in some sense to denigrate itself. By paying homage to its war dead it honors itself. By not allowing the loved ones of fallen heroes to lose heart, society bolsters its own courage. By legitimating their sacrifice and making it a bit easier to bear, society legitimizes itself in the eyes of its own citizens.

How is this to be accomplished? What is the nature of the institution that is to be an active agent in dealing with the bereaved and the psychologically wounded? Fundamentally, those institutions in modern societies available to deal with these issues are both bureaucratic and, in the case of the army, hierarchical. Both present problems.

BUREAUCRATIC HUBRIS AND HUMAN TRAGEDY

Peter Berger has taught us that it is the fundamental bureaucratic presupposition to assume "that there must be an appropriate agency and appropriate procedure for every conceivable problem in the bureaucratically assigned sector of social life." Applying this to the issue of bereavement, I believe that it is moral hubris to suppose that any social institution can formulate appropriate procedures to deal with every conceivable problem connected with the issue of death and bereavement. It is furthermore quite inconceivable that anyone could imagine it possible to formulate such procedures in the form of orders, so that subordinates in a hierarchical structure could or would obey them and successfully carry them out. The human potential for unanticipated response to fundamental life issues is limitless. To assume that one can foresee them all and provide standardized antidotes is itself a kind of nonhuman pathology.

To exemplify this I would like to quote from the draft of a publication submitted to the army hierarchy by a clinical psychologist who was justly concerned about the long-range effects on the notifier of bringing death notices to families. The concern is justified for, as Sophocles said long ago, "none love the messenger who brings the bad news." Such errands must have an effect on the self-image of the messenger. What does it do to their own anxiety when they bear such evil tidings to people and when they become a bureaucratically assigned and militarily commanded bearer of such woe?

The clinical psychologist was concerned about the messenger's fainting as a result of the deep anxiety that the situation could elicit:

What should the messenger do with himself—his inner life when he comes to the family? How should he prepare himself internally? The qualities that the informer generates should be compassion, softness and love. What should the messenger do when he feels inner pressure (anxiety)? He should not forget to breathe! He should attend to his own breathing and should breathe deeply and regularly. Breathing thusly should help in overcoming the anxiety (pressure). What should the messenger tell himself? (We all carry on an inner conversation with ourselves). It will help the messenger if he will tell himself positive things that strengthen him. That strengthen his belief that he conducted himself correctly and helpfully.

Unless these bits of friendly advice are meant in the most suggestive and tentative way they create visions of a judgmental dope (in Harold Garfinkel's phrase) who, in the process of disseminating compassion, softness, and love, is spending his time thinking positive thoughts and concentrating on breathing. It would constitute the grossest kind of caricature of military bureaucracies to imagine all that formulated in orders. The mind boggles at the thought of such a "dope" telling parents that the son has been killed.

If bureaucratic rules and orders cannot handle the existential complexity of the human predicament in extremis, what can? I believe that Berger has provided us with a way to see such tasks in the military. He calls the capacity of some bureaucracies to allow areas of humane spontaneity, *the capacity to structure actual eruptions of concrete humanity*. That capacity is based on the recognition by those in charge of the bureaucratic structure that one needs a respite from the rules in some extreme situations, from the idea that there is an appropriate procedure for every conceivable problem; that there is an appropriate agency; that it is possible to find someone competent to fulfill every function in the bureaucratic universe; that everyone can be fit into a category and thereby dealt with; that there are definable, definite procedures that can or should be applied to all situations; that individuals should be treated anonymously without distinction to their uniqueness.

I believe that the system that deals with fallen soldiers in Israel works because there is a very wise kind of a mix between bureaucratic regulation and the capacity of the system to structure possibilities of actual eruptions of concrete humanity. Every now and then in working one's way through the system as a bereaved parent, widow, or child one meets a real person. Furthermore, that person is allowed to be and to function within the bureaucratic structure in a way that allows him or her to actually get things done. In the cast of characters who are assigned parts in dealing with the bereaved, that person with the capacity for concrete humanity can both help the bereaved and help prevent the crises of legitimacy from erupting. Almost anyone dealing with the bereaved can fulfill that function. In one of the northern towns of Israel, the individual with the most standing in the community is the person who notifies families that their children have been killed. He does it in such a compassionate, feeling way that the relationships he forges with the families in their darkest hour frequently last. But such concrete humanity can erupt anywhere. It could happen with those who inform the families of the death or those who are assigned to be the masters of ceremonies at funerals, those who are providers of financial services on behalf of the defense department, those who are assigned to help families find a fitting memorial, those who are responsible for looking after the medical well-being of families, or those whose task it is to interpret the rules to the bereaved families. It can erupt anywhere. Where and when it does, great difficulties are avoided.

In writing about crises of legitimacy, George Kateb has defined them as follows:

deep and widespread feelings and opinions marked by disaffection from or hostility to the constitutive principles and informing spirit of the country's political arrangements . . . a legitimation crisis need not be a definite thing. It need not be a clearly manifested condition. It could exist without full explicitness, without people knowing how really disaffected or hostile they were. In the past, great political and social convulsions have sometimes come as a surprise to everyone, including the disaffected and hostile. Some incident or opportunity, or some quick sharp change in condition was needed to crystallize and then to energize the sentiments of crisis.

We have been arguing that the fallen soldier in general and the fallen soldier in Israel in particular constitutes potentially such a sharp change that can cause disaffection from constitutive principles of military organizations and societies. We have tried to maintain that, at least in Israel's case, the way in which the sudden change of the bereaved status is handled by the military, and which until now has prevented the crystallization and energizing of a sense of pervasive crisis, has been accomplished through the application of bureaucratic rules that allow for humane interpretation.

REFERENCES

Avinoam, R. *Deeds of Courage*, Vols. 1–12. Tel Aviv: Israel Defense Ministry, 1967 (Hebrew).

———. *Parchments of Fire: An Anthology*, Vol. 5. Tel Aviv: Israel Defense Ministry, 1970 (Hebrew).

Berger, P., B. Berger, and H. Kellner. *The Homeless Mind: Modernization and Consciousness*. New York: Vintage Books, 1973.

Cassell, E. J. "Being and Becoming Dead." *Social Research* 29, no. 1 (Spring 1972):537.

Demske, J. *Being, Man and Death*. Lexington, Ky.: The University Press of Kentucky, 1970.

Golan, A., and A. Shamir. *The Book of Valour*. Tel Aviv: Israel Defense Ministry, 1968 (Hebrew).

Kateb, G. "On the Legitimation Crisis." *Social Research* 46, no. 4 (Winter 1979):695–727.

Shapira, A. *The Seventh Day: Soldier's Talk About the Six–Day War*. London: Penguin Books, 1970.

Weiner, E., and A. Weiner. *Israel—A Precarious Sanctuary: War, Death and the Jewish People*. Lanham, Md.: University Press of America, 1989.

PART III

Commitment and Legitimacy Manifested and Measured: Nations and Organizations

These final four chapters are concerned with where we find commitment and legitimacy manifest in various military organizations here and abroad, how military service may be legitimated and rewarded, and how commitment to military service may be measured.

Claude E. Welch, Jr., suggests that military seizures of political power have become the functional equivalent of elections in many African states. With limited, fluid legitimacy, African governments and political leaders have been liable to frequent unconstitutional change. More than seventy successful coups d'état occurred between 1958 and 1986. In order to gain legitimation, both civilian and military regimes in Africa have stressed presidential power and leadership, have faced difficulties in achieving ethnic balance following governmental changes, and have been unmarked by significant economic growth or distribution. Given the high hopes of African leaders when independence was achieved, the brief length of self-government, and the economic and political shocks of the period, it may have been unrealistic to expect widespread legitimation. However, military authoritarianism compounds political inexperience and thereby impedes the legitimation of armed forces–dominated governments.

In Chapter 9, David Segal and Jere Cohen examine whether the right to demand fulfillment of the obligations of citizenship, such as military service in pursuit of the common defense, is the most important attribute of legitimate states. The three determinants of the legitimacy of military service obligations are the degree of threat perception, the equity of the distribution of the burden of military service across social groups, and the degree to which the fulfillment of citizenship obligations is related to the receipt of citizenship benefits. Educational benefits associated with military service can contribute to two of these: the equity of the distribution of the burden of service across the population and the degree to which those who serve are suitably rewarded.

This chapter reviews five phases in the exchange of educational benefits for military service in the United States: (1) the first two G.I. Bills, which rewarded conscription-era soldiers who served at less than market wages during the two world wars; (2) the Cold War G.I. Bill, which rewarded people for serving at less than market wages during peacetime; (3) the early years of the all-volunteer force when no G.I. Bill was in place; (4) the Army College Fund, which demonstrated that educational benefits could be used selectively as an enlistment incentive to bring high-quality personnel into critical military occupations; and (5) the New G.I. Bill, which used the valued symbols of the past to bring people into the military with contributory educational benefits.

This last program has been criticized for not being a cost-effective approach to recruiting personnel. Segal and Cohen concede this point and recognize that as military and civilian pay have converged in the all-volunteer force era, benefits other than pay have diminished in importance. However, educational benefits are seen to be making military service attractive to a broader range of the population, thereby increasing the equity of the distribution of military service. This equity, in turn, has contributed to the legitimacy of the military manpower system.

In his chapter, Wm. Darryl Henderson models cohesion as a product of organizational commitment, a condition fostered by nationalism. Quite naturally, different levels of nationalism in the countries examined produce uneven commitment (and cohesion) across these nation states.

According to this author, current explanations of why soldiers fight center on the concept of cohesion. Many have defined and described cohesion. Perhaps S.L.A. Marshal best captures the strength of cohesion and its core effect when he describes it as "one of the simplest truths of war . . . the thing which enables an infantry soldier to keep going with his weapon in the near presence or the presumed presence of a comrade."

Extensive research has made a significant contribution toward describing the characteristics and effects of cohesion and its importance in determining who wins a war. However, relatively little understanding has been developed to relate cohesion, a small-group phenomenon, to larger groups, such as a nation. Henderson points to the requisites necessary at this level for the creation of cohesive units that historically have added so much military power to the side that has best succeeded in marshalling the forces of nationalism.

The national population that supplies soldiers to an army also provides their beliefs and values. If soldiers in a small unit are from a relatively homogenous nation, the potential for strong unit cohesion and soldier commitment to group goals is likely to be enhanced. This chapter offers a method to identify the more important national characteristics that underlie a nation's potential for enhancing cohesive units and to measure their intensity. Historically, such characteristics have been evident in nationalism and the strong commitment of soldiers fighting in its various causes. Through the examination and comparison of the basic characteristics and related societal values underlying nationalism, the potential for creating cohesive units among the North Vietnamese, U.S., Soviet, and Israeli armies is examined and assessed.

In the final chapter of the book, Thomas Wyatt reports how commitment was measured empirically in a military organization. Membership commitment to U.S. Army Reserve organizations is hypothesized to be influenced by properties of the organization. This hypothesis was confirmed. Commitment, composed of group and individual variables, is analyzed from data collected from fourteen military reserve units geographically distributed throughout the United States.

Using contextual analysis, organizational factors are found to increase membership commitment more than do individual factors. Concepts of stability and voluntarism in organizations were found to be components of commitment and contributed to the explanation of that phenomenon. Contextual analysis, factor analysis, analysis of variance, and multiple regression were used to examine the data.

Wyatt contends that the military is more than a collection of individuals—it is a system of organizations—therefore, studies of military commitment must focus on the organizational setting rather than the individual.

8

Armed Forces and Political Legitimacy in Tropical Africa

Claude E. Welch, Jr.

Many recent observers of Africa have contrasted the high hopes at the time of independence with the actual gains that have been achieved. In the nearly thirty years since most of the states south of the Sahara have gained self-government, the gap between expectations and achievements has widened. Political aspirations—the assumption that self-determination would open the way to substantial gains in other realms—have not been matched by economic and social gains.

Severe financial problems date back to the 1970s. The OPEC price increases brought most African states ballooning balance of payments deficits and shortfalls in government revenues. Large-scale external borrowing alleviated difficulties in the short term, but intensified them in the long term. It is not uncommon at present to find debt servicing costs swallowing up half all foreign exchange earnings, leaving little if any for vital imports. Capital flight, repatriation of profits, declining exports, and corruption have negated most economic advances brought through external and internal investments and aid. Despite a special session of the United Nations General Assembly in 1986 devoted to the African debt crisis, effective solutions to the continent's economic development problems had not been found by the end of the decade.

These financial problems mirrored serious social issues. Significant expansions in schooling have created populations far more aware of what they lack relative to the more affluent parts of society, yet often without the requisite skills for meaningful employment. Creation of jobs continues to lag behind population increases. The demographic transition to reduced birth rates, a long-term consequence of urbanization, industrialization, and government policy, remains a distant dream. Food production has risen only marginally, due to the hammer blows of drought, insect infestation, questionable practices, and soil exhaustion in some areas. Population growth (especially in urban areas), government policies encouraging commercial crop exports rather than food production, and breakdowns in rural transport have more than counteracted gains brought by greater use of fertilizer and improved plant breeds in many countries. Countries that once exported substantial quantities of agricultural produce must now import a substantial portion of their food. The economic and social hopes of independence thus were too high for realistic fulfillment.

The aspirations for continental peace and progress that attended the birth of the Organization of African Unity (OAU) in 1963 remained largely unfulfilled by the late 1980s. A principal aim of the OAU was the elimination of external manipulation of African states; African solutions were to be found for African problems. The OAU sought to prevent both interstate and domestic conflict; should either erupt, the OAU would seek resolution. The situation was admittedly difficult when the OAU was created in 1963. Member states had achieved independence with frontiers drawn far more for colonial convenience than for socioeconomic rationality. Boundaries frequently sundered historic trade routes or divided ethnic groups among different European rulers; the resulting colonies had dubious economic viability and limited domestic integration. Nonetheless, the OAU was to protect the inherited status quo. These difficult objectives could not be fully achieved, as seemingly intractable political struggles confronted it: OAU's good offices could not, for example, resolve the Nigerian civil war in the late 1960s, nor could an OAU peacekeeping force in Chad restore effective governance in that strife-torn state in the early 1980s, nor for more than a decade could self-determination for the Saharawi people be squared with the Moroccan occupation of the former Spanish Sahara. The organization took a "see no evil" approach toward its members, neither directly investigating nor condemning acts in member states that cost hundreds of thousands of lives; on the other hand, the OAU took the initiative in drafting a continent-wide document on human and people's rights, which entered into force in 1987. Reiterated condemnations of South Africa, and vigorous efforts by presidents of the "front-line" states to reduce South African influence within their countries and to reverse the fundamental tenets of apartheid, appeared to bear little fruit, despite the U.S.- and UN-brokered steps toward the independence of Namibia. Indeed, even after pressuring Angola and Mozambique into nonaggression pacts in 1984, the Republic of South Africa continued its support of guerilla movements opposed to the incumbent governments of both; the encouragement of South Africa probably affected the military seizure of power in Lesotho in early 1986.

All these social, economic, and international issues took their toll on African leaders. Political life in many states south of the Sahara became a confused kaleidoscope of change, with instability and violence seemingly ever more prominent. Heads of state turned increasingly to authoritarianism, belying the initial hopes that independence would usher in wider popular participation in politics. Entrenching themselves in power, presidents rarely retired voluntarily; they died in the political saddle, sometimes naturally, sometimes by assassination or execution; far more often, they were deposed by the armed forces, in the absence of effective means for peaceful, effective shifts in leadership. Bullets rather than ballots became the most common means for choosing African heads of state. As can be seen in Table 8.1 at the end of this chapter, more than seventy changes of government personnel came about through coups d'état between 1958 and early 1989. The relatively small number of peaceful transitions under the auspices of a dominant party (i.e., from Senghor to Diouf in Senegal, from Ahidjo to Biya in Cameroon, from Kenyatta to Moi in Kenya) far outnumbered the popularly mandated changes of governing party (insofar as I am aware, only in Mauritius in 1982 did an opposition party or parties come to power through elections). In other words, as social scientists had started to glimpse by the late 1960s, military seizures of power have become the African functional equivalent of elections that shift power from one ruling group to another. The legitimacy any single government enjoyed is thus limited and fluid, seeming both to invite and to be reflected in continued instability in leadership.

This chapter focuses on the relationship between force and legitimacy. I do not ask directly whether the widespread prominence of the armed forces in ousting governments is a symptom or a cause of low political legitimacy; it is, of course, both. Far more interesting are the consequences of the current confused patterns of governmental change. What strategies could boost popular support for governments and political leaders south of the Sahara? In what ways might legitimacy be enhanced? What evidence is offered by recent African experience as to the relative effectiveness of civilian and military leadership?

It is far easier to delineate the factors that lead to military intervention in politics than the factors that lead to political legitimacy. In a valuable survey of reasons accounting for the dramatically broadened political role of armed forces in tropical Africa, Gus Liebenow gave prime attention to the weakness of nationalist parties. Their leaders' overestimation of their ability to control the postcolonial state; their underestimation of the role of force; their undermining of the bargaining context developed under colonialism; their increasing reliance on coercion; and their attempts to manipulate the armed forces to prop up their own tottering rule: such, in his judgment, were the crucial factors that led to military intervention in politics.[1] Seizures of power by the armed forces were the direct outcome of the weaknesses of the governing party. A vacuum at the political center resulted in the assertion of control by military officers. To consider the other side of the equation, David Goldsworthy stressed the need for "convergence" of effectiveness and legitimacy for civilian control of the military to endure. Specifically, he pointed to nine factors: manipulation of ascription, manipulation of psychological factors, manipulation of mission, payoffs, cooptation, political pluralism, military checks and balances, use of foreign patrons, and formal legal constraints.[2] To some extent, what establishes or maintains the politically subordinate role of the armed forces provides us with a start on what is requisite for political legitimacy.

Before reviewing the evidence, one initial caution must be noted. No neat, clear demarcation separates many "military" from many "civilian" regimes in tropical Africa. As John Ravenhill observed,

[To] classify regimes as military since their origins lie in a *coup d'état* serves to obscure the multitude of differences between "military regimes" on such characteristics as civil-military relations, ideology, political organisation, etcetera. . . . Military rule should be viewed as one manifestation of military intervention and influence on the political process. . . . The ideal-typical dichotomy drawn between civilian and military regimes has not been fruitful for theoretical analysis; in contemporary Africa it serves only to obfuscate the heterogeneity of political processes and regime types.[3]

Traditionally, of course, "civilian" governments achieve office through elections, "military" governments through coups d'état. The overwhelming majority of elections held under civilian auspices in postindependence Africa have confirmed the grip of the governing party and leader, as already noted; rare have been the occasions on which incumbents lost in balloting, and ever rarer those occasions on which victorious opponents have peacefully assumed power. Governments headed by civilians have been altered far more frequently by force than by fair elections; military seizures of power have become the most common form of political change in tropical Africa. As a consequence, many cabinets dominated by the armed forces have fallen victim to the same process that brought them to power: nearly a third of the successful coups d'état have been mounted against military juntas, as shown in Table 8.1 (see pp. 138–39).

In implementing policy, so-called military regimes have necessarily relied heavily on civilian allies—on bureaucrats, on traditional chiefs and notables, and on sympathizers who are usually drawn from the opponents of the deposed regimes. Conversely, several so-called civilian regimes have coopted members of the armed forces into the cabinet and have lavished funds and attention on the military to minimize the likelihood of intervention in politics. Most strategies seem not to work. Hence, greater attention has been given to deliberate encouragement of military participation in politics. African leaders and intellectuals, and foreign commentators as well, have spoken increasingly of the value of "diarchy," a deliberate mixing of those who have received the mantle of legitimacy by popular choice and those who have gained power from the barrel of a gun. Future political stability and greater legitimation depend, they argue, on mingling civilian and military sectors.[4] I believe the assertion is somewhat misdirected. The fundamental concern ought to be the process of legitimation itself. My intention here is to probe into the constraints that exist on building effective, legitimate political institutions, and to examine in particular whether leadership drawn from the military has any inherent advantage or disadvantage over civilian leadership in this process. Can officers serve as effective builders of political institutions in tropical Africa?

All governments in sub-Saharan Africa confront numerous difficult political choices. Their options are circumscribed by limited human and financial resources, rising popular demands, and norms of action that may stress personal and family enrichment more than national service. Indigenous traditions of political choice provide divergent models in multiethnic states. The authoritarian heritage of colonialism further complicates the choice of strategies. Should national leaders attempt to create a pan-tribal set of values, building thus upon domestic bases of support? Or should they draw more upon the coercive resources they enjoy to reduce opposition and establish more sweeping changes? Whatever choices may be made, African leaders must construct new patterns of political legitimacy. The following discussion examines several overlapping strategies for enhancing the support governments enjoy. Particular attention is given to states headed by military officers, recognizing the key role members of the armed forces exercise in many OAU member states. And, in considering approaches to legitimation, the discussion focuses on (1) potential advantages of military leadership in decision making, (2) issues of representativeness ("ethnic arithmetic"), and (3) problems of distribution, efficiency, and capacity, particularly through stimulation of economic growth.

POTENTIAL ADVANTAGES OF MILITARY
REGIMES

Military juntas enjoy an ability not as accessible to many civilian governments: the opportunity to legislate by decree. Acting in a quick, decisive manner, governing officers may not be as constrained as elected presidents in making tough decisions. Their no-nonsense manner of correcting long-standing grievances and problems appears to contrast with the muddle-through approach of civilians. For example, Yakubu Gowon could ordain the carving of four Nigerian regions into a dozen states in 1967, thereby largely eliminating a festering sore of that country's politics that civilians had ignored, and his successors Murtala Mohammed and Ibrahim Babangida could further slice them into nineteen and then twenty-one; Jerry Rawlings (Ghana) and Sammy Doe (Liberia) could send corrupt former politicians to the firing squad after the briefest of trials; Murtala could launch "Operation Deadwoods" to clear the bloated Nigerian bureaucracy of civil servants whose security of employment masked presumed inefficiency. Examples of this sort should not be overdramatized, however. Acting with authority is not the same as acting with despatch; governing authoritatively must not be confused with governing authoritarianly. The quick steps just cited may have been dramatic and popular, but were not wise in all respects.

In fact, many elected presidents in Africa have not been notably more constrained than coup-installed presidents in acting essentially without checks on their actions. Authoritarianism has marked men in mufti almost as much as their colleagues in khaki. Constitutions of all stripes have included provisions for emergency declarations of power; single-party control of legislatures has eased imposition of laws; a distinctively African style of leadership focused on the head of state has given presidents an enormous scope of action.[5] With the exception of draconian postcoup retribution (as in Ghana in 1979 or in Liberia a year later), contrasts in the nature of presidential actions based on the origins of the head of state have been limited. Idi Amin's expulsion of Asians from Uganda was paralleled by Busia's ouster of Nigerians from Ghana; the blatant grab of government resources by Jean Bedel Bokassa in the Central African Republic, and his self-proclaimed coronation as emperor, had more than a few similarities with the actions of many "presidential monarchs" elsewhere on the continent.[6]

The roots of centralized rule lie deep in the soil of tropical Africa. The period of colonial rule, brief as it may have been in the span of African history, significantly enhanced authoritarianism. European governments did not pursue policies devoid of any sensitivity to local conditions; on the other hand, their recognition and encouragement of democratic procedures on a national basis came well after World War II and were at best shallowly implanted in African soil. Colonial rule was neither representative nor democratic. Though it may have been presented as benevolent, it nonetheless denied rights of national political participation until close to the end of its life in Africa. The extensive powers exercised by African heads of state did not spring de novo from constitutions drafted at the grant of independence; they were based on ample colonial precedents.

In other words, civilian and military regimes in Africa have tried to legitimate themselves through an emphasis on presidential power and leadership, in remarkably parallel fashions. Styles vary, naturally, but there appear to be few consistent contrasts that can be ascribed to the immediate backgrounds of the heads of state. For almost every despotic president drawn from the military such as Amin or Bokassa, there has existed a counterpart such as Akwasi Afrifa (Ghana) or Sangoule Lamizana (Burkina Faso) willing to encourage political choice among contending groups. For almost every relatively moderate president drawn from civilian life who was willing to accept pluralistic choice, one could find a counterpart who denied any option other than his own party. Men in the first category, such as Dauda Jawara (Gambia) or Seretse Khama (Botswana), have been outnumbered by persons such as Kwame Nkrumah (Ghana) or Milton Obote (Uganda) who saw no acceptable alternative to their one-man, single-party governance. With the exception of the bloodletting that followed immediately upon some armed forces' seizure of power, and with the possible exception of some postcoup heads' of state willingness to decree immediate reforms, it is impossible to find consistent differences based on background or to ascribe contrasting policies to the particular training of the particular president. Strong leadership has emerged as the dominant style in postcolonial Africa, a trend to which officers and civilians alike have contributed.

Many postcoup governments have a basis for legitimation few long-term "elected" governments in Africa enjoy: They seize control with a list of grievances for resolution and may slice some Gordian knots that had reduced the legitimacy of deposed regimes. The simple fact of having removed a government with limited popular support provides a foundation of approval that can be built upon—at least temporarily. Of particular significance are commitments to return to the barracks, the disliked president having been ousted and the requisite reforms imposed. While civilian governments seek legitimation in their *initiation*, by campaigning for change prior to popular choice, some military-based governments seek legitimation in their *self-termination*, by opting to restore a sanitized regime. In this fashion, they carry out an implicit promise. One of the chief incentives to military displacement of civilian governments—or, alternatively, one of the chief grievances cited in postcoup rationalizations of seizures of power—has been the denial of political choice by the deposed group. The leaders of successful coups d'état in tropical Africa customarily cloak their personal and group aspirations in more grandiose terms. Their apologias for seizures of power often contain explicit promises about restorations of electoral choice. As A.H.M. Kirk-Greene has illustrated through his collection of documents,[7] the idea of reform followed by recivilianization is one of the most common themes. Civilians urge reform as part of preelection campaigning; officers promise redemocratization as part of postcoup rationalizing.

It is necessary to go beyond the rhetoric of postcoup apologias, however. What evidence exists that civilian and military governments in Africa pursue differing policies or achieve differential results in economic and social realms? In other words, is it possible to document systematic differences in policy effectiveness? Let us look at national representativeness and economic growth in greater detail.

ETHNICITY AND BALANCE

A second fashion in which legitimation can be enhanced is through balance and representativeness with government. Here, military juntas in Africa are pulled by opposing tendencies. On the one hand, they are likely to be highly homogeneous and narrow, as a consequence of the dynamics of coup plotting; on the other hand, they require a degree of popular and service branch support to govern effectively and, as a consequence, must become reasonably heterogeneous and broad. The initial necessity for exclusivity accordingly contradicts the subsequent necessity for inclusiveness. The result is a continuous tug of war within military ruling groups between conflicting objectives.

The risks and complexities of coup planning confine plotting to an inner group. Any successful seizure of power begins with a handful of disgruntled, ambitious individuals who seek change. Their need for secrecy almost inevitably makes the plotters suspicious of inquiries and prone to rely on each other with common experiences and perceptions. In the tropical African context, this frequently means shared ethnicity, in addition to such factors as training, postings, and other career markers that military sociologists have examined in documenting the causes and pathways of coups d'état.

The dynamics of successful governance, as already noted, pull in a different direction than the dynamics of coup-making. Hence, many successful military seizures of control south of the Sahara have been marked by an awkward pause between the ouster of the old and the installation of the new—a period to permit constituting a collective cabinet that is reasonably representative of branches of the military, regions of the country, and (more problematically) views within the armed forces. Such breadth makes eminently good political sense *after* the takeover, but little sense before it. Even when the coup coalition is broadened into a governing junta, problems remain, however. The most obvious strain within the ruling coalition occurs between the small circle of major planners and the surrounding circles of those brought in for balance and political clout. Those added at later dates obviously did not share the risks of, nor did they necessarily contribute to success in, the most difficult part of the coup, the action against the incumbents. Such latecomers would be expected to defer to the inner core. However, they may out-rank the initial plotters. Herein lies one of the chief reasons for the promotions members of the inner core bestow upon them-selves. And in breaching the considerations of seniority that affect promotion, ruling officers risk further disaffection within the military establishment itself.

I do not wish to imply that balance among different groups, regions, or backgrounds concerns only junta leaders. Analogous needs for breadth of representation mark civilian regimes in Africa as well. Indeed, the longest lasting of the party-dominated governments have persisted in part through their conscious bal-ancing of ethnic and regional interests. Relatively adaptable, open single-party systems (as exemplified, at various points in their history, by TANU/CCM of Tanzania, the PDCI of Côte d'Ivoire, or KANU in Kenya) have been inclusive rather than exclusive. Legitimation in tropical Africa depends to some de-gree on the breadth of the cabinet. Heads of state who narrow their circle of advisers to trusted persons from the same region, or who eschew ethnic arithmetic in their governments, find themselves with diminishing support.

One might argue that the "national" ethos of the armed forces facilitates breadth in any governing junta that may be created in sub-Saharan Africa. This view rests on a faulty premise. It assumes that the military, or at least the officer corps, contains a reasonable representation of major groups and regions. Rhetoric about the pan-tribal nature of officers' outlooks and training notwithstanding, the reality is that re-cruitment and promotion have been strongly influenced by ethnic factors. In the colonial period, barely a handful of Afri-cans advanced from the rank and file into noncommissioned officer ranks; commissionings of Africans were practically non-existent. Postindependence indigenization of the officer corps naturally favored those groups with significant numbers in the rank and file, from which some upward mobility became poss-ible after independence, but especially favored those groups with greater access to education and with links to the govern-ing party—or to the head of state. The upper echelons of the Zairean officer corps, for example, have come to be dominated by associates of Mobutu, drawn from the former Equateur region; senior Kenyan officers have increasingly become Kikuyu, although members of this group had been barred from recruitment into the military in the decade plus prior to independence. The upshot can be readily deduced. Ethnicity can become a bone of contention rather than a boon of contentment, as Kirk-Greene argued in the case of Nigeria.[8]

ECONOMIC AND SOCIAL CHANGE

Among the most common of observations in comparative politics has been the association among education, per capita wealth, and democracy. A well-informed, reasonably affluent citizenry, so it appears, can far more readily support a competitive, open political system than can an illiterate, village-bound, relatively impoverished citizenry—India notwithstanding. Governments that can "deliver the bacon" through promoting economic growth and distribution and a populace that can work effectively within political channels for change appear to be far less prone to military intervention in politics than poor states. Japan, North America, and Western Europe, accordingly, may have politically significant armed forces, but they also have peaceful changes of government without putsch or coup. In a related vein, highly organized party-states—Communist governments in which the military is clearly subordinated to the command of the party—face little danger of military seizures of power. Coups d'état have been concentrated in the Third World. Africa, much of Latin America, the Middle East, and most of South and Southeast Asia have been particularly prone to armed forces' intervention. In the period from 1958 to 1977, 157 coups d'état attempts occurred; none of these occurred in Communist countries, only six took place in Europe.[9] Following the above lines of reasoning, accordingly, we should look at the factors of legitimation contained within economic and educational growth, and in organizational factors. Unfortunately, time and space considerations preclude such an extensive inquiry. Instead, I shall ask only whether military juntas in Africa have had any greater success than their civilian counterparts in facilitating economic growth and social change, in other words, in promoting effective government performance in manners that might legitimate their regimes.

Using data from the mid–1960s to early 1970s, two American and two British political scientists classified states in Africa on the basis of the origins of the head of state—into civilian and military dominated governments—and examined various indicators of economic, social, and political well-being. One serious caution must be taken: The style of presidential leadership in Africa has reduced contrasts between the two types. A second warning flag must be raised about the quality of data: Although these scholars took great care to get the most accurate information, aggregate data from the south of the Sahara cannot always be accepted as correct. Third, particularly for the first scholar I shall cite, the information available on tropical Africa was quite limited. Sources of the data on the political role of the armed forces that stop in 1962 obviously suffer from serious deficiencies. These cautions noted, let us turn to the evidence.

Eric Nordlinger correlated seven indicators of modernization with the political strength of armed forces in order to determine whether governing officers were any more able than their civilian counterparts to enhance economic and social well-being.[10] In overall terms, he answered the question negatively: economic change was pursued only when the middle class was miniscule, while governments based on the armed forces showed only a permissive orientation to change rather than sustained efforts.[11] North African officers did not contribute to modernization, unlike their sub-Saharan colleagues; however, Nordlinger commented in a footnote that the positive correlations he found for tropical Africa were somewhat artificial, owing to data limitations.[12] The chief interests of ruling juntas seemed to lie in bolstering their corporate interests.

The British scholars R.D. McKinlay and A.S. Cohan focused on the period from 1961 to 1970, comparing military and non-military regime systems across twenty-five variables (e.g., political, military, background economic, international economic, and economic performance).[13] Through the use of partial correlations, multiple regressions, and cluster analysis, they divided 101 independent states (excluding Communist countries) into five groups. States in the first group (characterized by very low levels of political activity, high circulation of elites, and poor economic performance) tended to be governed by the military; states in the fifth group (characterized by very high levels of political activity and exceptionally high values on the background economic variables) tended to be governed by elected civilians; states in the fourth group fell mainly into the civilian regime group. In the second and third clusters, both military and civilian regimes could be found. No important differences in economic performance seemed to exist between types of regime; however, contrasts existed in the levels of both political activity (lower in military regimes) and political change (higher in military regimes).[14]

The most sophisticated quantitative analysis based on performance, in my estimation, was published by Robert Jackman.[15] He took seventy-seven countries in the decade of the 1960s, eliminating fifteen that had experienced more than one coup d'état. (His sample of African states was thereby reduced from twenty-seven to twenty-one.) Military intervention in politics, he discovered, had no unique effects on social change, regardless of either the level of economic development or geographical region.[16] Social change, contrary to Nordlinger's conclusions, varied with economic factors rather than in accordance with the military's political strength.[17]

Any analysis of governmental performance in sub-Saharan Africa must begin with a fundamental fact: scarcity of resources atop limited levels of development. No fewer than twenty-six of the thirty-six poorest states in the world are located in Africa. Monoculture economies have been whipsawed by declining world prices for many commodities and minerals and escalating prices for finished goods and many consumer products. States such as Nigeria that coasted for a while on escalating petroleum revenues have by now collided with the hard realities of international oversupply. Internal resources for investment are scarce, perhaps practically nonexistent. Heavy borrowing internationally has proven counterproductive, since insufficient foreign exchange exists for necessary imports as a result of debt servicing requirements. The dramatic slowdown in world trade as a result of the global recession of the early 1980s hit tropical Africa particularly hard.

The following statistics illustrate the magnitude of the problem. Ghana's foreign liabilities rose from 44 million cedis (1982) to 184.41 billion cedis (1987).[18] World prices for cocoa, the main export, fell more than a quarter, from a 1984 index of 105.32 to 73.61 in 1987.[19] Government deficits soaked up domestic resources and brought galloping inflation. In Zaire, for example, consumer prices rose from an index of 30 in 1982 (1985 being the base of 100) to 3,375 in August 1988.[20] Taking the continent as a whole, the average twenty-year growth rate (1965–1984) of 1.8 percent remained below the rate of population increase; the 1965–1973 rate of inflation, a relatively modest 4.2 percent, soared in the 1973–1983 period to 14.4 percent; food production fell to 94 percent of its 1974–1976 level by the early 1980s.[21] The continent's total indebtedness in 1970 of $5,426.2 million swelled to $58,828.7 million in 1984; in the same period, debt service jumped from $449.1 million to $7,425.8 million, far beyond what many states could pay.[22] To many, the "cure" seemed worse than the "disease." The bitter, deflationary economic medicine prescribed by the International Monetary Fund proved both politically unpalatable and economically uncertain in its consequences. Relatively stable, effective civilian governments (e.g., Cameroon, Côte d'Ivoire, and Kenya) were affected, including abortive coups d'état; economic woes atop blatant corruption spelled the end of Nigeria's second civilian republic, and the fiscal remedies and authoritarian attitude of the successor military government brought about its demise.

I am accordingly thus tempted to conclude on a relatively pessimistic note—but a note that affects all governments in tropical Africa. The expectations of independence were unrealistically high. Substantial achievements certainly have occurred, as Douglas Anglin has argued well,[23] and it would be unrealistic to anticipate that less than thirty years could implant widespread political legitimacy, generalized economic growth and improved distribution, and social integration. Stability based on governmental effectiveness and popular legitimacy remains a goal rather than an actuality. The steps that have been taken by African leaders offer no evidence that governments based on the armed forces have any greater success than governments based on civilians. The evidence I have surveyed here, if anything, tends slightly in the other direction. Their somewhat more authoritarian style atop their political inexperience or naiveté impedes legitimation. The task itself is difficult enough, given the limited economic, political, and social resources, but a disjunctive political process, punctuated by coups d'état and short-lived returns to the barracks, induces further problems. Force cannot bring stability; rather, legitimation gives the framework within which force can be appropriately exercised.

NOTES

This chapter is a revised version of a paper originally presented at a conference on Prospects for Africa, held in Stuttgart, West Germany, April 1986, under the sponsorship of the Defense Academic Research Program.

1. J. Gus Liebenow, "The Military Factor in African Politics: A Twenty-Five-Year Perspective," in *African Independence: The First Twenty-Five Years*, ed. Gwendolen M. Carter and Patrick O'Meara (Bloomington: Indiana University Press, 1985), pp. 129–40.

2. David Goldsworthy, "Civilian Control of the Military in Black Africa," *African Affairs* 80, no. 318 (1981), pp. 49–74, and, by the same author, "Armies and Politics in Civilian Regimes," in *Military Power and Politics in Black Africa*, ed. Simon Baynham (London: Croon Helm, n.d.), pp. 97–128.

3. John Ravenhill, "Comparing Regime Performance in Africa: The Limitations of Cross-National Aggregate Analysis," *Journal of Modern African Studies* 18 (1980), pp. 124–25.

4. See my chapter, "The Military and the State in Africa: Problems of Political Transition," in *The African State in Transition*, ed. Zaki Ergas (New York: Macmillan, 1986), pp. 191–216; for a critical view, see Arthur A. Nwankwo, *Civilianized Soldiers: Army-Civilian Government for Nigeria* (Enugu, Nigeria: Fourth Dimension Publishers, 1984), pp. 17–21.

5. Robert H. Jackson and Carl G. Rosberg, *Personal Rule in Black Africa: Prince, Autocrat, Prophet, Tyrant* (Berkeley: University of California Press, 1982).

6. Samuel Decalo, *Psychoses of Power* (Boulder, Colo.: Westview Press, 1989).

7. A.H.M. Kirk-Greene, *'Stay by Your Radios': Documentation for a Study of Military Government in Tropical Africa* (Leiden, Netherlands: Afrika Studiecentrum, 1980).

8. A.H.M. Kirk-Greene, "Ethnic Engineering and the 'Federal Character' of Nigeria: Boon of Contentment or Bone of Contention?" *Ethnic and Racial Studies* 6 (1983), pp. 457–76.

9. S.E. Finer, "The Military and Politics in the Third World," in *The Third World: Premises of US Policy*, ed. W. Scott Thompson (San Francisco: Institute for Contemporary Studies, 1975), pp. 66–67.

10. Eric A. Nordlinger, "Soldiers in Mufti: The Impact of Military Rule upon Economic and Social Change in the Non-Western States," *American Political Science Review* 64 (1970), pp. 1131–48.

11. Ibid., pp. 1142–44.

12. Ibid., p. 1146n.

13. R.D. McKinlay and A.S. Cohan, "Performance and Instability in Military and Nonmilitary Regime Systems," *American Political Science Review* 70 (1976), pp. 850–64; idem, "A Comparative Analysis of the Political and Economic Performance of Military and Civilian Regimes: A Cross-National Aggregate Study," *Comparative Politics* 8 (1975), pp. 1–30.

14. McKinlay and Cohan, "Performance and Instability," p. 862.

15. Robert W. Jackman, "Politicians in Uniform: Military Government and Social Change in the Third World," *American Political Science Review* 70 (1976), pp. 1078–97.

16. Ibid., p. 1096.

17. Ibid., p. 1086.

18. *International Financial Statistics* XLII, no. 3 (March 1989), p. 248.

19. Ibid., p. 82.

20. Ibid., pp. 572–73.

21. *Financing Adjustment with Growth in Sub-Saharan Africa 1986–90* (Washington, D.C.: International Bank for Reconstruction and Development, 1986), p. 67.

22. Ibid., p. 80.

23. Douglas G. Anglin, "Independent Black Africa: Retrospect and Prospect," *International Journal* 39, no. 4 (1984), pp. 481–504.

Table 8.1
Forcible Changes of Government in Africa, 1958–1986

Civilian Government Removed		Military Government Removed	
Date	Country	Date	Country
Nov. 17, 1958	Sudan		
Sept. 14, 1960	Zaire		
Jan. 13, 1963	Togo		
Aug. 15, 1963	Congo/Brazzaville		
Oct. 28, 1963	Benin		
Jan. 12, 1964	Zanzibar		
June 19, 1965	Algeria		
Nov. 25, 1965	Zaire		
		Nov. 29, 1965	Benin
Jan. 1, 1966	Central African Republic		
Jan. 3, 1966	Burkina Faso		
Jan. 15, 1966	Nigeria		
Feb. 24, 1966	Ghana		
July 8, 1966	Burundi		
		July 29, 1966	Nigeria
		Nov. 28, 1966	Burundi
Jan. 13, 1967	Togo		
Mar. 21-3, 1967	Sierra Leone		
		Dec. 17, 1967	Benin
		*April 18, 1968	Sierra Leone
Sept. 4, 1968	Congo/Brazzaville		
Nov. 19, 1968	Mali		
May 25, 1969	Sudan		
Sept. 1, 1969	Libya		
Oct. 21, 1969	Somalia		
		*Dec. 10, 1969	Benin
Jan. 25, 1971	Uganda		
**Jan. 13, 1972	Ghana		
May 18, 1972	Madagascar		
**Oct. 26, 1972	Benin		
July 5, 1973	Rwanda		
**Feb. 8, 1974	Burkina Faso		
April 15, 1974	Niger		
Sept. 12, 1974	Ethiopia		
		Jan. 25, 1975	Madagascar
April 13, 1975	Chad		
		July 29, 1975	Nigeria
Nov. 1, 1976	Burundi		
		March 18, 1977	Congo/Brazzaville
June 4-5, 1977	Seychelles		
May 5, 1978	Comoros		
		July 5, 1978	Ghana

Table 8.1 (continued)

Civilian Government Removed		Military Government Removed	
Date	Country	Date	Country
July 10, 1978	Mauritania		
		Feb. 5, 1979	Congo/Brazzaville
		Apr. 6, 1979	Mauritania
		*June 4, 1979	Ghana
Aug. 4, 1979	Equatorial Guinea		
		*Sept. 20, 1979	Central African Empire
		Jan. 4, 1980	Mauritania
April 12, 1980	Liberia		
May 11, 1980	Uganda		
Nov. 15, 1980	Guinea-Bissau		
Nov. 24, 1980	Burkina Faso		
Sept. 1, 1981	Central African Republic		
**Dec. 31, 1981	Ghana		
		Nov. 7, 1982	Burkina Faso
		May 18, 1983	Burkina Faso
		Aug. 4, 1983	Burkina Faso
**Dec. 31, 1983	Nigeria		
Apr. 23, 1984	Guinea		
		Dec. 12, 1984	Mauritania
		Apr. 16, 1985	Sudan
**July 27, 1985	Uganda		
		Aug. 27, 1985	Nigeria
Jan. 20, 1986	Lesotho		
		Jan. 27, 1986	Uganda
		Sept. 3, 1987	Burundi
		Oct. 15, 1987	Burkina Faso
Nov. 7, 1987	Tunisia		

Note: This table does not include abortive coups d'etat (such as in Congo/Brazzaville February 1972, The Gambia July - August 1981, Seychelles November 1981, Kenya August 1982, Central African Republic March 1982, Equatorial Guinea May 1983, Ghana June 1983, Benin April 1988 or Uganda October 1988). The coup d'etat in Transkei of December 30, 1987 has been excluded, given the questionable independence of that territory.

* = Coup d'etat intended to restore civilian government

** = Coup d'etat mounted against restored civilian government

9

Educational Benefits and the Legitimacy of Military Service

David R. Segal and Jere Cohen

The maintenance of a military force in a democratic state is dependent upon the willingness of the citizenry to serve. Any manpower policy can be effective only to the degree that citizens find military service to be acceptable, and are willing to serve, or have their progeny serve. This principle holds whether the military manpower system is based on conscription or voluntarism. Although military conscription involves a significant element of involuntary servitude, its success depends on its legitimacy. Like taxation, conscription is regarded as a claim that the state may legitimately make upon its citizens when, left to their own devices, the citizens would not fulfill this duty of their own volition. The recognition of this right to demand the fulfillment of obligations of citizenship may be the most important attribute of legitimate states.

Although the problem of legitimacy is present wherever military service is found, its magnitude varies with the type of manpower system. Due to the difficulty of justifying involuntary servitude in a democracy, conscription is more difficult to legitimize than a program of voluntary accession. In every war for which the United States raised military manpower through a national draft, there was opposition to the draft.

While conscription is more difficult to legitimize than voluntary service generally, it is easier to do so in wartime, when there are obvious and pressing national security needs, than in peacetime, when there is an absence of overt conflict. Thus, conscription, which has repeatedly been shown to be an effective instrument of wartime mobilization, may be less so for peacetime standing armies. This principle may help to explain America's adoption of an all volunteer force in 1973 (a step that had been taken briefly after World War II and contemplated after the Korean War as well); the more general trend toward voluntary military forces in the Anglo-American democracies; and ongoing deliberations regarding conscription in those western European nations that still maintain military drafts.

This trend away from conscription has been influenced by the fact that the weapons and transportation technologies available in the post-World War II world have deprived nations of the luxuries of time and distance from the battlefield that would allow them to mobilize for a major war. Denied the relative leisure of mobilization that was available in the past, nations have taken to maintaining large standing armies and navies in peacetime.[1] This has served as a force for military voluntarism, and against conscription.

This is not to say that perceptions of national needs for conscription are absent among democratic nations. There is, for example, a sufficient threat to the security of Israel to justify, in the mind of its public, a system of (almost) universal conscription. Similarly, the borders of the Federal Republic of Germany are perceived by a sufficiently large proportion of the German population to be vulnerable enough to maintain conscription as a viable military manpower policy there. However, the same sense of vulnerability to an invading force is not pervasive in America.

The end of the U.S. draft removed certain legitimacy problems associated specifically with conscription but did not eliminate the problem of the legitimacy of military service entirely. The legitimacy problem is different with a volunteer force than with a draft, but this only means that the justification of service must change.

THREE DETERMINANTS OF LEGITIMACY

There are (at least) three determinants of the legitimacy of military service. First, as argued and illustrated above, the degree of threat perception is a determinant of the acceptability of military service in a democratic state. This factor is particularly crucial for justifying a system of conscription.

A second determinant is the degree to which the manpower system distributes the burden of military service equitably across various sectors of the citizenry. The equity problem arises from the inequality of personal sacrifice which is inevitable when some serve while others do not, some see combat while others do not, and some are killed, disabled, or wounded while others are not. Equity is most closely approached when no one is required to serve, or when the military manpower system mobilizes a large proportion of the population at risk, as exemplified by the widely (but not universally) accepted drafts in the United States during the two world wars and the Korean police action. The more complete the mobilization, the more equal the distribution of danger and disadvantage and the greater the degree of equity. Conversely, the smaller the proportion of the population at risk that is actually called to serve, the greater the breach of equity.

Furthermore, the larger the proportion of the citizenry inducted, the greater the likelihood that the armed force will be broadly representative of the population, and hence, the burden of sacrifice equitably shared not only among individuals, but among social strata. The drafts during the world wars and the Korean conflict were acceptable not only because so many sacrificed, but also because of the way in which the sacrifice was distributed: the armed forces in these wars were seen as broadly representative of the citizenry, the exclusion of women from all three and the racially segregated nature of the American military during the first two notwithstanding.

In contrast, the drafts during the Civil War and the Vietnam War were opposed at least in part because, like the militia system that served as the forerunner of conscription in America, they were perceived to have significant socioeconomic biases and did not distribute the burden of military service broadly among the citizenry. The all-volunteer force of the 1970s was likewise controversial because it was not socioeconomically representative.[2] It continued gender biases at a time when women were claiming increased citizenship rights and responsibilities, and it placed the burdens of service disproportionately upon the black community, which had only recently won expanded citizenship rights through the civil rights movement.

A third determinant of the legitimacy of a military manpower policy is the degree to which a fair exchange relationship exists between the citizen and the state. The costs incurred by individuals in fulfilling their obligations of citizenship must be perceived to be offset by citizenship benefits. These benefits may be collective or individual.

Collective benefits appear greatest during wartime, when military victory and the preservation of national security are obvious rewards. Collective reward is less obvious in times of peace. The success of deterrence and the maintenance of peace seem to be less tangible and satisfying rewards than the success of battle and the defeat of the enemy. They certainly are not celebrated by parades and the bestowal of social honor.

During peacetime, when only a minority of the eligible must serve even in a large standing force and the benefits of national security (which is a public good) are not obvious, the rational position for the individual is to let someone else provide that good, unless other rewards are forthcoming. He will then be a recipient of a generally available benefit at no cost to himself. The lower or less apparent the collective benefits of mobilization, the more important individual rewards become to those who serve. This maximizes the importance of the exchange relationship between the individual and the state.

When military service seems equitably distributed, legitimacy problems are minimized, and exchange benefits are relatively unimportant as legitimizing agents. Conversely, to the degree that the principle of equity is breached, the exchange relationship between the individual and the state becomes more important. The history of military pensions illustrates this point. As the distribution of pension benefits increasingly diverged from the principle of equity over time, these benefits increasingly became rewards to individuals for their service. Initially, following the principle of equity, the benefits were designed to reflect degrees of sacrifice. Thus, prior to the Civil War, military pensions were primarily compensation for war-related disabilities or survivors' benefits. It was only as the Civil War mobilization cohort aged that the definition of disability was broadened to include old age, and the principle of equity was breached as we ceased to differentiate among those who had been wounded in combat, those who had served in combat, and ultimately those who had simply served.[3] A distinction was maintained, however, between those who had served and those who had not.

In sum, both the inadequacy of collective benefits and the presence of inequity heighten the need for legitimation through individual exchange value. It has been primarily in peacetime, and in the absence of mass mobilizations, that nations have sought to identify tangible benefits for those who have served in the military.

MILITARY EDUCATIONAL BENEFITS

Our concern in this chapter is with the effect upon legitimacy of an important benefit of military service: educational assistance. It is our thesis that educational benefits can contribute to two determinants of the acceptability of a military manpower system: the equity of the distribution of military service across the population, and the degree to which those who have served are suitably rewarded.

Educational benefits linked to military service have gone through five phases in America, each of which has affected the balance of the exchange relationship between the service person and the state, and the most recent of which have affected the equity of the distribution of the burden of service across the citizenry. Through both relationships, these benefits have affected the legitimacy of the military and its means of manpower accession.

The first phase was represented by the first two G.I. Bills, which recognized service in wartime by people who were frequently brought into the military by processes of conscription, either as draftees or as "draft motivated volunteers." These people had not only been exposed to the risks of war, but had been paid less than a market wage for doing so.

The second phase was the Cold War G.I. Bill, which recognized that service in the standing force that we maintained after Korea, although it did not put service people in harm's way, did represent service at less than a market wage, as well as an interruption in education or career development. The second phase was transformed by historical accident—a peacetime G.I. Bill became a wartime G.I. Bill as a result of increased American involvement in Vietnam.

The third phase was the "no G.I. Bill" period of the all volunteer force. If the G.I. Bill had been meant to equitably reward service that was particularly dangerous (wartime), or involuntary (conscripted), or at less than a market wage, then a volunteer force, in peacetime, with pay scales calibrated to civil service pay, did not require educational benefits (the fact that such benefits can be an important enlistment motivator aside).

The fourth phase was the introduction of the Army College Fund, which demonstrated effectively that enhanced educational benefits would bring higher quality personnel into critical occupations in the armed forces. And the fifth stage is the new Montgomery G.I. Bill.

Phase One: The First Two G.I. Bills

Like military pensions, educational benefits associated with military service were initially an after-the-fact reward to personnel who had served, and thereby sacrificed, in wartime. At the end of World War II, the nation faced the demobilization of millions of young men who would flood the labor force of an economy only recently recovered from the Great Depression; who would be junior in terms of job security and educational attainment to their peers who had not served in the armed forces during the war; who might resent being economically disadvantaged because they had served their country; and who might challenge the legitimacy of the sacrifice that they had been asked to make. In response, the United States established a massive program for the education and training of veterans at government expense: the Servicemen's Readjustment Assistance Act of 1944, or the original G.I. Bill.

This educational benefit program did achieve its objective. Almost eight million World War II veterans—more than half of the total eligible population—received training under this first G.I. Bill, reducing pressure on the employment system and improving the veterans' competitive position in the labor force. A second Veteran's Readjustment Assistance Act was passed in 1952 for veterans of the Korean police action, and over 2 million veterans—about 43 percent of the eligible population—participated in training programs under this support. These bills covered a period of service when higher education was not widespread in America, and educational benefits did seem to equitably offset the lost wages and time incurred by veterans.

Phase Two: The Third G.I. Bill

In 1966, a third act was passed to cover personnel who served at least 180 days during the post-Korea Cold War and who received honorable discharges. This was the first G.I. Bill explicitly intended primarily to provide benefits for veterans who did not serve during wartime, although it ultimately did cover veterans of the Vietnam War. The Vietnam experience notwithstanding, the definition of sacrifice required to receive educational benefits had changed under the law, from having served in wartime to simply having served. More than a million veterans of the Cold War period—about 46 percent of the eligible population—were trained under this G.I. Bill, as were almost 7 million Vietnam-era veterans—a record 72 percent of the eligible population. However, as we shall see below, the Vietnam-era veterans did not profit as much relative to their peers who did not serve as did their predecessors, due in part to the increased availability of educational benefits not tied to military service.

Research which compared veterans to their peers who did not serve in the military has demonstrated that prior to the Vietnam War period veterans received higher levels of education than nonveterans, and that much of the difference could be credited to G.I. Bill educational benefits.[4] In the early 1950s for example, only between 14 and 15 percent of young adults were enrolling in institutions of higher education, a figure lower than the percentage of veterans using the G.I. Bill to attend colleges and universities. These differences in turn were reflected in differences in postservice income in the civilian labor market. This is consistent with the frequently demonstrated effect of higher education on status attainment.[5]

Some economists have suggested that military service has a negative impact on civilian earnings because military service delays or interrupts civilian careers.[6] This is precisely the kind of effect that the framers of the first G.I. Bill sought to avoid, and the evidence suggests that they were in the main successful during the pre–Vietnam War period. A series of studies have shown that veterans from the World War II and Korean War periods earn more than their nonveteran counterparts, other things being equal. These positive effects are greatest for groups that have been disadvantaged in the civilian labor market: blacks, Hispanics, and women.[7] Thus, military service can be thought of as contributing to the subsequent welfare of veterans in general and veterans who are members of disadvantaged groups in particular. Their service to the state has been rewarded.

The picture changes with regard to Vietnam-era veterans. Vietnam veterans have had the highest rate of G.I. Bill utilization of all veteran groups. As noted, over 72 percent of Vietnam-era veterans utilized their educational benefits, compared to 50 percent or less of the earlier veteran groups. Moreover, a far greater percentage of Vietnam-era veterans used their benefits specifically for college education rather than for other kinds of training than did earlier veterans. More than 45 percent of Vietnam-era veterans used their benefits for college, as compared to 15 percent of World War II veterans, 22 percent of Korean War veterans, and 24 percent of post–Korean War veterans. Yet Vietnam-era veterans, although better educated than veterans of earlier wars, achieved less education than their peers who did not serve, and thus did not achieve an advantaged position in the civilian labor force. Their educational benefits did not offset the costs of their absence from civilian careers during military service.[8]

While the utilization of G.I. Bill educational benefits has grown over time, apparently rewarding those who have fulfilled the citizenship obligation of military service, the growth of benefits not tied to service has grown more rapidly, providing greater potential rewards for those who have not served, thus upsetting the equilibrium that had been established in the exchange relationship between citizen and state.

Military veterans of World War II and the Korean War returning to civilian society in America prior to the 1960s reentered a system in which welfare programs, including educational assistance, were a relatively small part of the federal budget, despite their short term growth during the depression. Federal expenditures for welfare programs had fallen from about half the budget in 1935 to less than a third in 1955. In 1950, about 30 percent of expenditures for social welfare were accounted for by veterans' programs, and veterans' educational programs accounted for about half of all federal funding for education. Higher education was still the exception rather than the rule in the young adult population, and G.I. Bill benefits were a major source of grant support for higher education.

In the early 1950s, about one half of one percent of the federal budget was devoted to educational programs not associated with military service. More than 7 percent was allocated to veterans' programs. The G.I. Bill was a major element of the American welfare state during this period. Expenditures for veterans' benefits exceeded nonveteran federal expenditures for health, education, housing, and community development through the decade, but the trend was toward nonmilitary programs. By 1960, veterans' programs had declined to 10 percent of public welfare expenditures, and civilian educational programs had increased to 34 percent.

The decade of the 1960s saw continued change in this direction. Spending priorities were shaped not only by the war in Vietnam, which would eventually wind down, but also by the War against Poverty and by President Lyndon Johnson's quest for a Great Society. Previously neglected segments of society, some associated with the movement against the Vietnam War, sought access to expanded citizenship rights and entitlements, including educational assistance. Educational expenditures were increased in response to bellicose international pressures as well. Advances by the Soviet Union in technologies with military applications led to domestic educational programs, such as the National Defense Education Act of 1954, which were intended to contribute to national security by upgrading the technological capabilities of the nation through provision of support for civilian higher education in science and other defense-related fields.

The percentage of the young adult population attending college more than doubled between 1953 and 1969. Between 1935 and 1973—the first year of the all-volunteer force—federal expenditures for educational assistance not tied to military service had been increased twenty times. In 1973, when conscription was ended, veterans' programs were 6 percent and civilian educational programs were 30 percent of public welfare expenditures. In terms of federal support for education as a benefit of citizenship, the nation had produced "The G.I. Bill without the G.I."[9] Far more assistance for higher education was available without requirements for military service than was available through educational benefits associated with military service; if one was in need of government assistance for higher education, the opportunity costs of military programs were higher than those of nonmilitary programs.

Although veterans of the Vietnam era were more likely to receive G.I. Bill benefits than were veterans of earlier wars and although they achieved higher levels of education than did veterans of earlier wars, they were the first group of veterans to fail to keep pace educationally with their peers who did not serve in the military. The costs to career development and job seniority that were associated with their military service were not offset.

Our research on men who had been surveyed in 1957–1958 while they were in high school, and who were resurveyed in 1973, showed that although the military veterans in our sample, most of whom had served during the Vietnam War, were fairly well educated, they averaged a year less education than their peers who had not served in the armed forces.[10] The difference could not be attributed to social background characteristics or to processes of selection or self-selection for military service. Even with the existence of a G.I. Bill, the Vietnam-era veterans in our sample were unable to catch up educationally to their peers who had not invested time in military service and who had access to educational entitlements not dependent on such service.

We did find that the educational disadvantage of Vietnam-era service was restricted to enlisted personnel. Officers in the aggregate were neither educationally advantaged or disadvantaged by their service, relative to their peers who did not serve. The disadvantage was restricted to the great majority of armed forces personnel who serve in the enlisted grades and who tend to come from the lower socioeconomic strata of society. While enlisted personnel who entered the military without high school diplomas were likely to finish high school while in service, only a small proportion did college-level work either while in service or thereafter, and they ended up with less schooling than their nonveteran peers. Officers, by contrast, were likely to finish baccalaureate degrees or begin graduate studies while in service, to continue their higher education after service, and to catch up or stay even with their civilian peers.

The educational disadvantage of Vietnam-era veterans seems to have had implications for their earnings, relative to that of their nonveteran peers. As noted above, veterans of prior wars had been advantaged with regard to both education and income relative to nonveterans. Early research on the civilian earnings of Vietnam-era veterans, based upon the 1970 census, suggested that this was no longer the case: Vietnam veterans were shown to have sustained significant income penalties as their reward for service.[11]

It is of course possible that by 1970 Vietnam veterans would not yet have had time to offset the time lost in service, but that they might eventually do so. However, more recent research, based upon data from 1977—four years more recent than our own educational attainment data—show the income penalty, although diminished, to still exist and to be unlikely to disappear. For the first time, nonwhite veterans were not advantaged relative to nonveterans. And surprisingly, the one group of male veterans that did experience an income increment relative to its nonveteran counterpart was the least educated: veterans who entered the military without a high school diploma and who did not take advantage of in-service or postservice opportunities to finish their high school level work.[12] Equally ironically, female veterans of the Vietnam War period, whose contribution to the war effort had been minimized as a matter of policy, also experienced increments in civilian earnings relative to their non-veteran peers.[13]

To sum up, Vietnam-era veterans did not, for the most part, experience educational or occupational advantages to compensate them for their sacrifice. Despite the G.I. Bill, the exchange between veteran and state was disadvantageous to the G.I. Since the collective benefits of the Vietnam War were elusive and controversial, and since participation in that war was unequally distributed in terms of race and social class, it is particularly damaging to the legitimacy of that war to recognize that its veterans were penalized materially for their service. Serious legitimacy problems contributed to the challenges to the military manpower system in effect at that time.

Phase Three: The All-Volunteer Force

G.I. Bill educational benefits were discontinued in 1976, the third year of the all-volunteer force. A volunteer force that paid a fair market wage for service was presumed to impose a lesser degree of sacrifice on those who served than had conscription, and noncontributory educational benefits were not seen as a cost effective recruiting incentive. A contributory program, the Veterans Educational Assistance Program (VEAP), was established in its place, but it was neither very popular nor very successful in bringing higher mental aptitude personnel into the armed forces.

Research prior to the establishment of the all-volunteer force had demonstrated the importance of educational benefits as an enlistment incentive for brighter young men, producing a broader balance in both ability and ideology among military recruits.[14] However, the recruiting strategies in the early years of the all volunteer force had regarded college-bound youth as unlikely prospects.[15]

In the absence of an attractive package of educational incentives, the representation of personnel with higher education (and with aspirations for higher education) dropped in the armed forces. Morris Janowitz and Charles Moskos note that, while in 1964, prior to the Vietnam War, 13.9 percent of army *enlistees* had some college, the volunteers of the 1970s were less highly educated. In 1977, when about 29 percent of American males aged 19 or 20 had some college, only about 5 percent of nonprior service army volunteers had that level of education.[16] In the navy, the percentage of all personnel who had some college dropped from 26 percent in 1972 (the last year before the all-volunteer force) to 10 percent in 1976.

Unfortunately, caps placed on civil service pay during the 1970s as a means of minimally controlling the federal deficit caused entry level military pay to once again lag behind market wages and yielded recruiting shortfalls. While the army was able to meet its numerical recruiting objectives in the early years of the all-volunteer force, it experienced recruiting shortfalls in 1977, 1978, and 1979—the three years after the expiration of the G.I. Bill. Personnel quality also declined. VEAP was not particularly useful in overcoming these problems for two reasons: the low military pay level made it difficult for junior enlisted personnel to take up to $100 a month out of their pay as a contribution, and it did not carry the valued label "G.I. Bill."

While there has been relatively little substantial social research on the status attainment of early veterans of the all-volunteer force, initial indicators are that they, like the Vietnam-era veterans before them, are having greater difficulty establishing themselves in the civilian labor market than their peers who did not serve. The *Wall Street Journal*, for example, reported a 9.7 percent unemployment rate among post-Vietnam veterans, compared to an overall rate of 7.2 percent.[17]

An early concern of critics of the all-volunteer force had been that the enlisted ranks, rather than drawing on a cross-section of the citizenry, would recruit disproportionately from the lower educational and social strata of society. This raised both practical and moral considerations. Would a force with low levels of education be able to handle the machinery of modern warfare and provide America with national security? Was it fair to ask the segments of the population that received relatively little of the benefits of society to bear most of the burden of military service?[18] Would the middle class, if not called upon to help man the armed forces, become estranged from the military institution? Would a military drawn increasingly from a restricted range of the social structure become increasingly militaristic?[19]

One of the costs of not having a G.I. Bill was that the middle class—many members of which had been educated under earlier G.I. Bills—kept its sons and daughters home from the service. This raised the problem of equity—the distribution of the burden of national security in the population under no-draft conditions. The problem was exacerbated by the increased availability of educational benefit programs not requiring military—or any other—service. For example, National Defense Education Act benefits and guaranteed student loans were aimed largely at middle-class youth.

Phase Four: The Army College Fund

In the decade of the 1980s, research began to demonstrate that even in the ground combat forces, which historically had disproportionately recruited lower educational personnel, brighter, more well-educated soldiers were better soldiers.[20] Rather than continuing to regard college-bound youth as an infertile recruiting field, the army began to court the college bound. In 1981 the army initiated the Army College Fund, whereby personnel in the higher mental aptitude categories who enlisted in critical military specialties—primarily in the combat arms—could earn appreciable educational benefits. Between 1980 and 1981, the percentage of high school graduates among army nonprior service recruits increased from 54 percent to 80 percent. By 1985, it had increased to 91 percent.

This not only served to bring in the quality of personnel that the services felt that they needed but, given the rising costs of higher education, it also made service more attractive to middle class youth with college aspirations, thus enhancing equity. However, it still left the military at a competitive disadvantage relative to other educational entitlement programs, which did not require military service as a condition of receiving benefits.

Phase Five: The New G.I. Bill

With the cost of higher education in America escalating, the widespread availability of educational assistance programs not tied to military service placing the armed forces in an increasingly disadvantaged position in competing for higher mental aptitude personnel, and the size of the military age–eligible cohort decreasing each year as the baby-boom generation passed its prime military entrance age, a new G.I. Bill was established. President Reagan had opposed such a plan through his first term, but members of Congress who disagreed with the president convinced him that the Defense Department's appropriation for Fiscal Year 1985 would move more smoothly if the White House agreed to a new G.I. Bill. On July 1, 1985, new G.I. Bill educational benefits were established on a three-year experimental basis.[21] Like VEAP it was a contributory program. Personnel participating in it were required to contribute $100 a month for the first year, and this money would not be refunded if they did not get civilian education or training. Unlike prior G.I. Bills, it was intended not to reward past service, but to attract future recruits. The nature of the exchange relationship had once again changed.

The new G.I. Bill achieved immediate popularity. During its first three months over 70 percent of the eligible soldiers signed up for it (compared to about 50 percent participation in VEAP during that program's most successful years). Over half of the soldiers who signed up for the new G.I. Bill during this period also participated in the Army College Fund. These soldiers will accumulate up to $25,200 in educational benefits in exchange for up to four years of service. This program has experienced high popularity in part, we believe, because it carries a label valued by the parents of today's military age–eligible youth.

Given projected decreases in other educational entitlement programs, continued increases in the cost of higher education, and declining sizes of high school graduating classes into the 1990s, the new G.I. Bill could be the program that bridges the gap between the military and the middle class that the Vietnam War produced. As a consequence, it could distribute military service in American society more equitably. Alternatively, like other federal educational benefit programs, it might fall victim to presidential infanticide. The president's budget for Fiscal Year 1987, issued six months after the initiation of the authorized three-year experiment, and in the face of increasing personnel quality, noted: "Because the Secretary of Defense has determined that this program is unnecessary for recruitment, the administration is proposing legislation to terminate this costly test program as of October 1, 1986, and reopen the post-Vietnam era education program [VEAP]." The Congress disagreed. We would argue in favor of the continuation of the new G.I. Bill, on the grounds that it will enhance the legitimacy of military service.

We agree that an educational benefit program available to all recruits is not a cost-effective approach to recruiting personnel in the higher mental aptitude categories. And we concede that that the importance of benefits other than pay are of diminished importance to the exchange between service person and state in a volunteer force paying competitive market wages; the legitimacy issue has not hinged on exchange since the end of phase two. However, as exchange has diminished in importance as a determinant of legitimacy, the equity problem has increased, and it has remained unresolved. Although it may well be unnecessary to address directly the role of benefits in the exchange process now (a situation that may change if pressures toward a balanced budget depress military wages), there is no obvious way to enhance equity while leaving exchange untouched. If the new G.I. Bill is aborted, neither equity nor exchange relations will benefit, and the legitimacy of military service is likely to be injured. If the bill is continued, equity, exchange, and military legitimacy will all be enhanced.

NOTES

1. Morris Janowitz, *Military Conflict* (Beverly Hills, Calif.: Sage, 1974), p. 121, and David R. Segal and Mady Wechsler Segal, "Change in Military Organization," *Annual Review of Sociology* 9 (1983), pp. 160–61.

2. Morris Janowitz and Charles C. Moskos, "Five Years of the All-Volunteer Force: 1973–1978," *Armed Forces and Society* 5, no. 2 (Winter 1979), pp. 171–218.

3. David R. Segal, "Military Personnel," in *American Defense Annual 1985–86*, ed. Joseph Kruzel (Lexington, Ky.: D.C. Heath, 1986).

4. Neil D. Fligstein, *The G.I. Bill: Its Effects on the Educational and Occupational Attainments of U.S. Males 1940–1973*, Working Paper 76–9

(Madison, Wis.: Center for Demography and Ecology, n.d.), and William M. Mason, "On the Socioeconomic Effects of Military Service," Ph.D. diss., University of Chicago, Department of Sociology, 1970.

5. Peter M. Blau and Otis Dudley Duncan, *The American Occupational Structure* (New York: Wiley, 1967).

6. W. L. Hansen and B. A. Weisbrod, "Economics of the Military Draft," *Quarterly Journal of Economics* 31 (1967), pp. 395–421, and Walter Y. Oi, "The Economics of the Draft," *American Economic Review* 57 (1967), pp. 39–63.

7. Melanie Martindale and Dudley L. Poston, Jr., "Variations in Veteran/Nonveteran Earning Patterns among World War II, Korea, and Vietnam War Cohorts," *Armed Forces and Society* 5 (1979), pp. 219–43; Wayne D. Villemez and John D. Kasarda, "Veteran Status and Socioeconomic Attainment," *Armed Forces and Society* 2 (1976), pp. 407–20; and Dudley L. Poston, Jr., Mady Wechsler Segal, and John Sibley Butler, "The Influence of Military Service on the Civilian Earnings Patterns of Female Veterans," in *Women in the United States Armed Forces*, ed. Nancy L. Goldman (Chicago: Inter-University Seminar on Armed Forces and Society, 1984), pp. 152–71.

8. Jere Cohen, David R. Segal, and Lloyd V. Temme, "Military Service Was an Educational Disadvantage to Vietnam-Era Personnel," *Sociology and Social Research* 70 (April 1986), pp. 206–8.

9. Charles C. Moskos, "Making the All-Volunteer Force Work, *Foreign Affairs* 60, no. 1 (Fall 1981).

10. Jere Cohen, David R. Segal, and Lloyd V. Temme, "The Educational Cost of Military Service in the 1960s," *Journal of Political and Military Sociology*, 14 (Fall 1986), pp. 301–19.

11. Villemez and Kasarda, "Veteran Status and Socioeconomic Attainment."

12. Mark C. Berger and Barry T. Hirsch, "The Civilian Earnings Experience of Vietnam-Era Veterans," *Journal of Human Resources* 10, no. 4 (1983), pp.455–79.

13. Poston, Segal, and Butler, "The Influence of Military Service."

14. Jerome Johnston and Jerald G. Bachman, *Youth in Transition*, Vol. V: *Young Men and Military Service* (Ann Arbor, Mich.: Institute for Social Research, 1972).

15. Martin Binkin and John D. Johnston, *All-Volunteer Armed Forces: Progress, Problems, and Prospects*. Report prepared for the Committee on Armed Services, United States Senate, Ninety-Third Congress, First Session (Washington, D.C.: U.S. Government Printing Office, 1973).

16. Janowitz and Moskos, "Five Years of the All-Volunteer Force."

17. Toni Joseph, "Rude Awakening: Many Veterans Find Service No Road to Success," *Wall Street Journal*, October 9, 1985, p. 22.

18. Janowitz and Moskos, "Five Years of the All-Volunteer Force."

19. Jerald G. Bachman, John D. Blair, and David R. Segal, *The All-Volunteer Force* (Ann Arbor: University of Michigan Press, 1977).

20. Barry L. Scribner et al., "Smart Tankers Are Better Tankers," *Armed Forces and Society* 12, no. 2 (1986), pp. 193–206.

21. David R. Segal and Nathan L. Hibler, "Manpower and Personnel, Policy in the Reagan Years," in *Defense Policy in the Reagan Administration*, ed. James Brown and William Snyder (Washington, D.C.: National Defense University Press, 1988).

10

Societal Effects on Soldier Commitment in the Vietnamese, U.S., Soviet, and Israeli Armies

Wm. Darryl Henderson

Common attitudes, values, and beliefs among soldiers in a unit can promote individual soldier commitment to the unit, its leaders, and the mission of the unit. The absence of common values and beliefs makes the formation of a cohesive combat unit with strong soldier commitment to the unit extremely difficult. Some observers hold that the presence of common values and attitudes, more than any other factor, contributes to strong soldier commitments[1] and the absence of such similarity holds the potential for intraunit conflict, especially if the group is held together by authority from outside the group.[2]

The national population that supplies soldiers to an army also provides at the same time their beliefs and values. Soldiers in small units (primary groups) are drawn from an overall population or secondary group which can be defined as the pattern of impersonal relationships within a large organized group.[3] A secondary group such as a nation is much too large to function on the intimate face-to-face basis of a cohesive primary group

EDITOR'S NOTE: The author ties cohesion to nationalism and commitment to cohesion throughout this chapter. The result is a stretched model of commitment and a novel way of looking at commitment and legitimacy. In the discussion of the potential for nationalism in the United States, the author's comments on race are addressed almost exclusively to the military subculture.

yet it provides the requisite values and beliefs that in large part make the creation of the small group with strong member commitment possible. Therefore, if soldiers in a small unit are from a relatively homogeneous secondary group or nation, the potential for strong unit cohesion and soldier commitment is likely to be enhanced. On the other hand, dissimilar secondary group characteristics within a unit such as language, religion, race, history, and the values that accompany these characteristics tend to hinder the development of strong soldier commitment to the unit.

Much recent research and writing both in the United States and abroad, primarily in Israel, has measured and described soldiers' commitment to each other, their units, and the organizational purpose or unit mission in terms of mutual bonding or "cohesion." This research has been very useful because for the first time it allows reliable measurements of individual and small-group norms that exist within a unit and which control the day-to-day behavior of the soldier and the degree of commitment with which the soldier fights.

Not as easily measured but generally recognized as having significant influence on the development of soldier commitment to a unit are the broader set of characteristics and cultural values inherent to a nation that impart common attitudes, values, and beliefs among the soldiers in a unit. Beginning in 1848, with the advent of nationalism, historians have noted that, for the first time, armies, raised among people over wide geographical regions in support of commonly held values perceived as legitimate, fought with greater commitment. To the degree such national characteristics and values are evident in a secondary group such as a nation these values can impart a legitimacy to a common purpose which, to the degree these values are common to all soldiers in a unit, can contribute significantly to a soldier's commitment to his unit and his will to fight.

The existence of national characteristics and values that, because of their legitimacy within the secondary group, provide the potential to develop soldier commitment can be found at three levels: (1) at the national level in terms of broad descriptive characteristics which provide the basis for nationalism, (2) within the culture or subcultures and related values inherent to a nation and, (3) within policies and practices that enhance the commonality of soldier values within the organization of an army. The presence and the intensity of the characteristics, values, and beliefs associated with the three levels outlined above can be determined. Offered below is a subjective and broad, but also useful, method for assessing the strength of the national characteristics and values available to a nation and upon which it can build strongly cohesive units with strong soldier commitment to unit and mission.

NATIONALISM AS A BASIS FOR SOLDIER COMMITMENT

Significant research has been accomplished on the relationships among the commonality of national characteristics, the phenomenon of nationalism, and the ease with which cohesive armies have been created among nations experiencing nationalism.[4] Nationalism may be defined as follows: "A belief on the part of a large group of people that they constitute a community called a nation, that is entitled to independent statehood and the willingness of that people to grant their nation their primary terminal loyalty."[5] The degree to which a strong commonality of such attitudes, values, and beliefs can be demonstrated between large secondary groups and much smaller primary groups will indicate the ease with which small cohesive military units can be created in a society.[6] A nation's potential for nationalism and thereby the existence of the basic values and beliefs necessary for soldier commitment within military units may be determined through an investigation of the following characteristics of a nation.

Two primary requisites for nationalism are an adequate population and the amount of territory a state controls or aspires to control. Another significant factor contributing to nationalism is a group's sense of a common and unique history and shared values. Generally, a people's history is a source of common values. It will be a force that draws a people together, especially if it includes a significant period of trial such as fighting and winning a revolutionary war or a war in defense of its boundaries. Even more significant is a people's expectation of a common future. Such a history rapidly becomes part of a people's culture. Legends and historical tales become part of every citizen's socialization. The telling and retelling of these experiences by teachers, grandparents, and friends perpetuates a group's history and also passes on cultural values to new generations.

A common language also promotes nationalism. It eases communication among people for a wide variety of purposes, and it also establishes firm boundaries that often distinguish the group from others. A sense of belonging to a unique group or race, often with an accompanying religion, also contributes to nationalism. Consider the Iranian resurgence of national pride and unity with its emphasis on the Persian heritage and Islamic religion.

Leadership, too, is an extremely important nationalistic factor. It is essential that the nation is the primary loyalty among the elite of a people. An elite or leadership with loyalties divided between transnational parties, specific geographical regions, or particular ethnic groups or tribes within the larger secondary group is a significant hindrance to the emergence of nationalism and ultimately to cohesion in that nation's army.

The final indication of a group's potential for nationalism is affected by all of the preceding indicators. It is the degree to which the overall population is aware that they are part of a nation and the priority they give that nation.

In sum, a nation's potential for nationalism and ultimately for cohesion in its army is indicated by the degree to which the following are present:

1. A large enough population
2. Sufficient territory
3. A common and unique history
4. A common and unique culture
5. A common language
6. A common religion
7. A common race
8. A nation that is the primary loyalty for the elite

9. An adequate percentage of the population that is aware of the nation and give it a primary loyalty

Just a bare outline of the principal factors affecting a nation's potential for nationalism has been presented here. The detailed work of Rupert Emerson, Hans Kohn, and Richard Cottam makes clear the degree to which nationalism is rooted in the basic cultural characteristics of a nation and supports the thesis that common cultural values significantly promote cohesion among members of a small unit. The following section contains a comparative assessment of the requisites for soldier commitment provided by the characteristics and cultures of four nations. The descriptions are all in summary form and roughly current except for the section on Vietnam which describes the North Vietnamese Army (NVA) of the Vietnam War.

Potential for Nationalism in Vietnam

Population: With a population approaching 50 million, the Vietnamese are certainly numerous enough to form and maintain a nation.

Territory: With approximately 127,000 square miles, Vietnam has sufficient territory. Geographical diversity, with two distinct climates and highlands and lowlands, could be a source of vulnerability. Vietnam is 1,400 miles long, 39 miles wide (at the 17th parallel).

A Common and Unique History: Dating from 208 B.C., Vietnam has had a history of constant struggle against foreign domination (Chinese and French), internal rebellion, and expansive wars to the south into the lands of the Champa and Khmer.[7]

A Common and Unique Culture: There is a strong sense of cultural heritage. The oral history passed from generation to generation not only perpetuates but strengthens the sense of a common heritage and values that positively affect cohesion. Ellen Hammer describes how minstrels carry in song the past of the nation, the value of independence, and the exploits of its favorite heroes.[8]

A Common and Unique Language: In the nineteenth century, a new and even more distinctly Vietnamese writing system (*quoc*

ngy), which relied upon a romanized translation of spoken Vietnamese, was adopted throughout the country. A new language was introduced into Vietnam by Vietnamese intellectuals and helped to distinguish the Vietnamese from all surrounding people.[9]

A Common and Unique Religion: Vietnamese religious culture is diverse—Confucianism, Taoism, Buddhism, and Christianity. Religion has not strongly enhanced the potential of nationalism in Vietnam.[10]

A Common and Unique Race: The Vietnamese have a strong sense of belonging to a unique race. They trace their origins to 500 B.C., when several clans living in the Yangtze River region of China decided to migrate south to the Red River delta and farther after coming under strong pressure from the Chinese to assimilate.[11] Approximately 15 percent of the present population is not considered to be Vietnamese. These include highland aborigines, overseas Chinese, Chams, and Khmers who occasionally came into conflict with the dominant Vietnamese.[12]

Primary Loyalty of the Elite for the Nation: It appears that Vietnamese soldiers see their immediate leaders as nationalists rather than as Communists. The typical North Vietnamese soldier was not aware of any other midrange or top Communist party leader other than Ho Chi Minh. In addition, squad, platoon, and company leaders usually explained the necessity of fighting the South Vietnamese and the Americans in terms of Vietnamese nationalism.[13]

Vietnamese People's Perception of Vietnam as a Unique and Viable Nation: The Vietnamese are aware of the Vietnamese nation and its uniqueness. A popular legend in Vietnam concerns Le Loi, a national hero who led the Vietnamese to freedom from the Chinese. Part of the legend, quoted below, was made popular by the Vietnamese poet Nguyen Trai and is learned by most Vietnamese children: "Our people long ago established Vietnam as an independent nation with its own civilization. We have our own culture. We have our own mountains and our own rivers, our own customs and traditions, and these are different from those of the foreign country to the North [China]."[14]

Potential for Nationalism in the United States

Population and Territory: As one of the largest countries in the world, having a population of well over 225 million, the United States is well suited for nationalism.

A Common and Unique History: U.S. history is a strong source of common values for the American people. The strong socialization process has reinforced these values. American participation in World Wars I and II and the Korean War appears to represent a high point of confidence held by the people in the American Way. The war in Vietnam, however, with accompanying foreign policies, has created considerable doubt among the citizenry and government about the reasons and methods of dealing with foreign nations. Such questioning of the legitimacy of U.S. foreign policy significantly detracts from American potential for nationalism.

A Common and Unique Culture: Although American culture is pluralistic—primarily a blend of Judeo-Christian English and European cultures—most citizens feel and support values that can be described as uniquely American. High among these values is the sense of worth in being an American and a basic loyalty toward and respect for American institutions, among which are the armed forces and their missions.

A Common and Unique Language: Because English is so widely spoken and understood throughout the United States, ease of communication is facilitated among American soldiers and significantly promotes cohesion. Two recent societal trends, however, appear to work against ease of communications within the small unit and, to some degree, hinder cohesion and commitment. First, significantly lower reading and comprehension skills have forced the army to rewrite many manuals and other directives to tenth grade and below levels of comprehension. Second, some minority soldiers do not possess sufficient English skills to allow them to become integrated fully into primary groups—a problem that hinders cohesion and commitment, especially if there is also reluctance to learn and use English.

A Common and Unique Religion: The broad umbrella of Christianity that covers most religions in the United States offers some basis for common religious values, which in turn promote the basic values necessary for cohesion. Diversity in values among Christian beliefs in America and also among other religions and their respective leaders can be significant sources of conflicting values capable of hindering a consensus about national values and related military and foreign policies.

A Common Race: Within the U.S. Army, racial conflict between whites and blacks currently is not significant. Ease of communication and general agreement about basic values appear to provide a working consensus among black and white soldiers that supports national values and promotes cohesion. In some units where the percentage of black soldiers is significantly disproportionate, however, reservations are heard on two counts. First, these units are usually combat units; hence, black casualties would be disproportionately higher in the event of war. Second, some evidence suggests that when the proportion of blacks in an organization rises above 10 to 15 percent, racial friction increases significantly.[15] All this suggests that, although racial conflict in the U.S. Army is manageable, the possibility of significant conflict is not remote.

Another ethnic situation that might become more significant for the U.S. Army is the growing Hispanic population in the United States and its distinctly procommunity, nonmilitary tradition and its Spanish-speaking values.

Primary Loyalty of the American Elite for the Nation: The great majority of the American elite would generally state that the United States is a primary loyalty. When this loyalty is translated into specific areas, however, support for a military tradition is at best fragmented, a fragmentation that represents lack of a unifying military ethos within American society.[16]

The nature of America's fractured consensus about what constitutes a proper civic consciousness is paraphrased in the following composite view of several widely respected observers and commentators:

A breakdown in the cultural legitimacy of the American system has been an object of scholarly analysis and commentary. That a significant section of the American intellectual and media establishment oppose the basic outlines of American foreign policy is a fact of immense importance. It is not that they disagree on technical details, but that they believe the United States is on the wrong side of history . . . political leaders, corporation executives, law enforcement agencies, ranking military officers—have displayed an increasingly cynical if not outright negative tone. An insightful content analysis of American history textbooks in high schools shows an important break in tradition, where formerly a coherent picture of American history was presented in terms of a unified nation, occurred in the 1950s. The social portrait since the 1960s has been one that is fragmented and lacking a core theme. Research findings on elite attitudes also present a picture of a divided and somewhat confused, national leadership. If in fact the national elite has no unified consensus about civic consciousness, it may be asking too much to expect it of our soldiers.[17]

American Perception of the United States as a Unique and Viable Nation: The great majority of Americans have a strong and common cultural heritage within which the concept of an American nation is strong and widespread. Unifying myths and values are plentiful and widely accepted.

Potential for Nationalism in the Soviet Union

Population and Territory: As the largest country with a population of approximately 270 million, the Soviet Union possesses sufficient territory and people to serve as the necessary foundations for nationalism.

A Common and Unique History: Because a common history is the source of many unifying values, the impact of the various histories of the peoples currently comprising the Soviet Union makes for mixed influences upon the potential for nationalism within the Soviet Union today. In 1917, when the Soviet Union came into existence, it assumed responsibility for what in effect was a Tsarist colonial empire consisting of many peoples with unique histories. Forces toward disintegration were significant. It was not until World War II, called The Great Patriotic War by the Soviets, that a real basis for a unifying and common history became apparent for the majority of Soviet citizens. Hedrick Smith makes the point: "What makes World War II so valuable . . . is that it lends itself to blurring the distinction between the devotion of ethnic Russians to Mother Russia and the attachment of minority nationalities to their own regions. It allows propagandists to meld these peoples together in common loyalty to the broader entity of the Soviet Union."[18]

A Common and Unique Culture: Within the Soviet Union, the 1979 census determined there were 102 "Soviet nations and nationalities," or separate cultures. All are subject to the draft and military service. Beginning in 1967, the Soviets decided to emphasize "compulsive military service linked to the Russian language as a means to create a cultural melting pot." This is a significant and difficult task. Not only do the 102 separate nations represent different cultures, but in many cases they represent a past history of armed conflict against the majority Russians. In 1917, most non-Russians attempted to break away from the Bolsheviks, but the Russians maintained the old Tsarist empire by force. The Bolsheviks, however, were forced to organize a federal state system that recognized some differences among the "nations" that constitute the Soviet Union.[19] Subsequent Soviet attempts to break down cultural barriers among the various nations and to promote the Russian language and culture as the desired model have, however, achieved some success. The potential for nationalism among the 14 million Russians and some closely related Slavic cultures appears to be great. Smith comments: "Russians are perhaps the world's most passionate patriots. Without question, a deep and tenacious love of country is the most unifying force in the Soviet Union, the most vital element in the amalgam of loyalties that cements Soviet society."[20]

A Common and Unique Language: Within the Soviet Union, there are sixty-six separate languages. Many of these were unwittingly instituted by the Soviets themselves in an earlier attempt to separate Soviet ethnic groups from ethnically similar groups and movements beyond Soviet borders. Soviet attempts to make Russian the primary language within the Soviet Union have shown some gains. Largely because of army efforts, between 1959 and 1979 the number of non-Russians who use Russian as their primary language rose from 13 to 16.3 million and Russian as a second language rose by 46 percent. As a result, 82 percent of the Soviet population is reported to know Russian.[21] Soviet potential for overall nationalism is significantly limited, however, because the great majority of the population still use their native tongue as their primary language. During the past twenty years the percentage who use their native tongue has dropped by only 1 percent, from 94 to 93 percent.

A Common Religion: Religion in the Soviet Union, despite official persecution and expropriation of church property, remains a significant influence on Soviet culture. Within Russia, the Orthodox church appears to be healthy. Baptisms are increasing and estimates are that approximately 30 to 50 million Russians are Orthodox Christians, significantly more than are Communist party members.[22] Moslem influence still supports separate identities among the Soviet peoples. Religion cannot be considered a common and unique characteristic.

A Common Race: In the Soviet Union, race follows the general pattern described above for culture and languages—that is, races are many, varied, and they are strong sources of differing values and of conflict, especially within those Soviet Army units that have been chosen to be "agents of national integration." It appears that a major racial cleavage has evolved between Slavs and Asians within the Soviet Union and especially within the armed forces. The list of derogatory terms used in the Soviet Army to refer to members of other races is long; the words have extremely disparaging connotations. At the root of this racism are deeply held Russian biases toward other races.

Among the various nationalities that make up the Soviet Union, race can be an extremely strong force for nationalism within the various separate nations, especially among the Russians and other Slavs. But the great diversity of races within the Soviet Union today is a major obstacle for a pan-Soviet nationalism. This argues against easy achievement of commitment in Soviet military organizations.

Primary Loyalty of the Elite for the Soviet Union: Major problems exist here also, since the patterns of perceived trust among Soviet leaders generally follows that of race, language, and culture. Russians are encouraged to migrate to the minority republics and assume positions of key leadership in the government and economy. Within the army, the leadership is overwhelmingly Slavic. Ukrainians are strongly represented within the NCO corps, and the officer corps is 95 percent Slavic and 80 percent Russian. Non-Slavs are discouraged from pursuing leadership careers.[23] Overall, it appears that the Soviet elite is divided on critical issues that affect the potential for Soviet nationalism.

Soviet People's Perception of the Soviet Union as a Unique and Viable Nation: In a country where almost one-half the population does not use the official language as its primary language and where the strongest loyalties are reserved for particular ethnic cultures, the overall perception of the uniqueness and viability of the Soviet Union must be considerably less than that desired by the Soviet leadership. There are clearly problems of divided loyalties that must be faced by Soviet leadership. Soviet leaders have not forgotten the large numbers of defections in minority nationalities to the Germans during World War II, but they find the process of shifting primary loyalties of national minorities from their own cultures to the Soviet state exceedingly difficult.

Potential for Nationalism in Israel

Population: Because Israel has a population of about 4 million surrounded by a hostile Arab population of about 300 million many observers have expressed concern for Israel's survival as a nation.

Territory: Not including the disputed territories, Israel consists of about 8,000 square miles. Much of this territory is arid and therefore not useful for agriculture or other purposes. Also important is the fact that key military terrain (such as the Golan Heights and the West Bank) is not now included within Israel's claimed boundaries. Occupation of this key terrain by opposing military forces could be a significant threat to Israel.

A Common and Unique History: One of the strongest traditions among the Jewish people is their common and unique history. One thousand years of national independence, followed by the 2,000–year Diaspora after the Jews were exiled from Babylon, produced a strong Jewish identity and a latent desire to return to their "promised land." "Next year in Jerusalem" became a rallying cry among Jews wherever they were found throughout the world. For nearly 3,000 years, the fragmented Jewish "nation" grouped around their spiritual leaders, the rabbis, the Torah, and the Talmud to preserve their common beliefs. It was not until after the *Dreyfus* case in France, however, that the modern Zionist movement began and that Jews started to return to the promised land with a reawakened spirit of nationalism. When World War II, with its great disruption of peoples worldwide and Nazi persecution of the Jews, provided a major impetus for Jewish immigration to Palestine, Jews from around the world acted out their centuries-old dream of returning to the promised land. From wherever the new arrivals came, they already had in mind a belief in their common and unique history. It was a major factor in promoting a strong feeling of nationalism in the newly formed State of Israel.

A Common and Unique Culture: Today, approximately 50 percent of Israeli citizens are native born, or sabras.[24] Because the remaining 50 percent have come from almost all the separate Jewish groups represented in the Diaspora, the effects on Israeli culture have been significant. Most of the newcomers were Sephardic Jews from the Middle East and North Africa, whose cultures varied from sophisticated and well-educated Egyptian Jews to cave-dwellers from the Atlas Mountains. The largest group not from northern Africa came from Iraq. Others arrived from Turkey, India, Syria, Lebanon, and other scattered locations. Their common denominator was unfamiliarity with Western institutions, especially with concepts of democratic government.[25]

The Ashkenazi, or western Jews, came mostly from Europe. The largest group emigrated from Poland, but sizeable numbers also arrived from Romania, the USSR, Germany, and Austria; fewer numbers migrated from most other European states.

A Common and Unique Language: Language also has a mixed effect on Israel's potential for nationalism and, consequently, military commitment. Spoken by most Israelis, Hebrew is the most widely used language in Israel. Arabic is also a national language, spoken by many Sephardic Jews. English is taught in the schools and widely understood. Yiddish is frequently used by many Ashkenazic Jews. The fact that almost all males serve in the defense forces significantly promotes Hebrew as a common and unique language—a potent force for nationalism, cohesion, and, ultimately, commitment.

A Common and Unique Religion and Race: Judaism is the predominant faith, but there are also sizeable Muslim and Christian communities with a smaller number of Druzes. The greatest religious conflict, however, appears to be within the predominant Jewish community between Orthodox and other, more secular Jews. The root of the problem appears to be conflict between the very strict religious laws that emerged during the Diaspora, which allowed the Jews to survive as a unique people, and the distinctly different secular requirements of running a nation-state. When the army was first formed, many in the Orthodox community demanded that two armies exist, one that would observe the religious laws and another that took a more lax position.[26] Compromise and the threat of Arab invasion have produced an army that has substantial religious law written into its regulations yet not to the degree that essential defense measures are ignored. Again, it appears that the army, through necessity, is an instrument of religious integration, making Judaism an even more powerful influence for Israeli nationalism.

Primary Loyalty of the Elite for the Nation: While the Israeli system of government is a parliamentary democracy with parties in opposition to the government in power, there is a broad and powerful consensus on the rules governing the uses and purposes of power.[27] Foremost is the defense and survival of Israel. All internal cleavages one would expect to find in the extremely heterogeneous Israeli population and political parties are subordinated to this one objective. The overriding priority given by all members of the Israeli elite to the defense of Israel, no matter what their background or the constituency represented, is a major promoter of both Israeli nationalism and cohesion in the Israeli Defense Forces.

Israeli People's Awareness of Israel as a Unique and Viable Nation: The people of few nations other than Israel demonstrate in their day-to-day actions the awareness of their nation and the dangers that it faces. Historically, the perception of an imminent and significant threat has usually caused heightened nationalism. Because of their long struggle and tragic history, the Jewish people are even more sensitive to outside threat. With the formation of the State of Israel, a concrete entity came into being that has served since as the object of overwhelming loyalty.

Israeli Perception of Israel as a Unique and Viable Nation: When assessed and compared, as shown in Table 10.1, vulnerabilities

Table 10.1
Potential for Nationalism

Element	North Vietnam	United States	Soviet Union	Israel
A large enough population	+ +	+ +	+ +	+
Sufficient territory	+ +	+ +	+ +	+
A Common and unique history	+ +	+ +	+	+ +
A common culture and language	+ +	+	- -	+
A common religion	-	+	-	+ +
A common race	+	-	- -	+
Nation is primary loyalty of elite	+	+	+	+ +
Degree of population aware of and loyal to nation	+ +	+ +	+	+ +

Legend: Strong + +

         +

         -

  Weak   - -

in national characteristics become apparent. The vulnerabilities reflected in this table could significantly affect the capability of each nation to form any units with strong soldier commitment to their units and their mission.

CULTURAL VALUES AS A BASIS FOR SOLDIER COMMITMENT

The individual soldier's commitment to broad cultural values inherent to his society, such as the values that govern the economic or political systems, and to their underlying ideology, such as democracy or communism, appears to contribute to the legitimacy felt by the soldier toward the "system" he is defending. Such commitment to the values of a sociopolitical system is often characterized by broad and general statements by a soldier that his governmental system is best. In support of his belief, the soldier usually points to evidence of the felt inherent superiority of his sociopolitical system. Examples often cited are the obvious and plentiful material goods of Western capitalism or the classless societies of communism. Such attitudes can further explain a soldier's behavior if they reflect a perceived need to protect the system through actions against another system or ideology (such as anticommunism or anti-imperialism). Through his concept of "latent ideology" Charles Moskos suggests that broad cultural values can influence a soldier's behavior and commitment and states that soldier beliefs "must therefore be taken into account in explaining combat performance."[28]

The reasons soldiers fight, of course, cannot be reduced to one particular reason—neither to small-group cohesion explanations nor to broader, fighting-for-a-cause explanations which are based in culture or ideology. As Morris Janowitz stated, "Obviously, we are dealing with an interaction pattern, but the primary group is essential for the realities of battle. If there is no social cohesion at this level, there is no possibility of secondary symbols accomplishing the task."[29] Effective leadership, especially confidence in the commander at company level, often outweighs any question about the legitimacy of the war during combat.[30] It appears that secondary group values have their greatest impact on soldier commitment when they are internalized by the soldier through the small unit that incorporates these broad societal norms directly within its day-to-day operations. In this instance, the cultural value loses much of its "empty-slogan" character for the soldier and is linked directly to small-group rules and expectations about his behavior and action. Possibly more than any other army, the North Vietnamese Army succeeded in combining the broadest national values with the basic day-to-day rules that governed behavior in the NVA and resulted in strong soldier commitment toward national goals.

In addition to broad societal norms, more specific cultural and subcultural values which reinforce the soldier's perception that society sincerely values his service and sacrifices also contribute strongly to soldier commitment. Societies that value soldiers reinforce the romanticism and manly honor often seen in the soldier's life by members of society, especially the youth. This value is perpetuated through tradition and ceremonies honoring the military. Materially, societies that value military service provide soldiers priority and special privileges in obtaining the good things a country has, such as special stores and financial aid for education and housing.

In sum, the potential for cultural and subcultural values to reinforce soldier commitment to his unit through the perceived legitimacy of the system he is helping to defend is manifest through societal values and programs similar to the following:

1. The soldier's belief that his nation's political system is the best as result of socialization or indoctrination

2. Evidence of the superiority of their system, such as the material well-being of the West or the classless society of communism

3. A felt need by the soldier to protect the system through actions against another system (such as anticommunism or anti-imperialism)

4. Broad cultural values and norms that have been internalized by the soldiers and become operating norms of the small unit

5. The romanticism and manly honor often seen by youth in the soldier's life through tradition and society

6. Special programs to provide soldiers priority and special privileges for the good things in a society

NOTES

1. E.P. Hollander and R.G. Hunt, eds., *Current Perspectives in Social Psychology* (New York: Oxford Press, 1963), pp. 298–311.

2. Wm. Darryl Henderson, *Cohesion, The Human Element in Combat* (Washington, D.C.: National Defense University Press, 1985) p. 75.

3. Alexander L. George, "Primary Groups, Organization and Military Performance," in *The Study of Leadership* 11 (West Point, N.Y.: USMA Printing Plant, 1973), pp. 20–23.

4. John Biesanz and Mavis Biesanz, *Modern Society* (Englewood Cliffs, N.J.: Prentice-Hall, 1968), pp. 91–93.

5. This definition of nationalism and the accompanying criteria for measuring its potential are taken largely from a series of lectures delivered by Professor Richard Cottam at the University of Pittsburgh during the summer of 1969. In arriving at this definition Professor Cottam built on the ideas of Hans Kohn and Rupert Emerson. See Hans Kohn, *Nationalism, Its Meaning and History*, rev. ed. (Princeton, N.J.: Van Nostrand, 1965), and Rupert Emerson, *From Empire to Nation* (Boston: Beacon Press, 1967).

6. George, "Primary Groups, Organization and Military Performance."

7. Roy Jumper and Marjorie Weiner Normand, "Vietnam: The Historical Background," in *Vietnam: History, Documents and Opinion*, ed. Marvin E. Gentleman (New York: Fawcett, 1965), pp. 10–28.

8. Ellen Hammer, *Vietnam, Yesterday and Today* (New York: Holt, Rinehart and Winston, 1966), pp. 220–21.

9. Douglas Pike, *Viet Cong, The Organization and Techniques* (Cambridge, Mass.: MIT Press, 1966), p. 374.

10. Hammer, *Vietnam*, p. 39.

11. Pike, *Viet Cong*, p. 2.

12. Ann Crawford, *Customs and Culture of Vietnam* (Tokyo: Tuttle, 1968), pp. 55–61.

13. Henderson, *Why the Vietcong Fought* (Westport, Conn.: Greenwood Press, 1979), p. 53.

14. Hammer, *Vietnam*, p. 1.

15. Martin Patchen, *Black-White Contact in Schools: Its Social and Academic Effects* (West Lafayette, Ind.: Purdue University Press, 1982), p. 349.

16. Morris Janowitz, Letter, February 22, 1983.

17. Charles C. Moskos, "Civic Education and the All-Volunteer Force," paper presented at the IUS symposium on Civic Education in the Military, October 15–16, 1981, p. 21. See also James N. Rosenau

and Ole R. Holsti, "U.S. Leadership in a Shrinking World: The Breakdown of Consensus and the Emergence of Conflicting Belief Systems," *World Politics* 35 (April 1983), pp. 368–92.

18. Hedrick Smith, *The Russians* (New York: Ballantine Books, 1980), p. 405.

19. Andrew J. Rochells and Paul G. Patton, "Demographic Changes in the U.S.S.R.: Implications for the Soviet Military," student paper, (Washington, D.C.: National Defense University, 1982), p. 29.

20. Smith, *The Russians*, p. 404.

21. Rochells and Patton, "Demographic Changes in the U.S.S.R.," p. 20.

22. Robert G. Kaiser, *Russia, The People and the Power* (Brattleboro, Vt.: Book Press, 1976), p. 83.

23. Rochells and Patton, "Demographic Changes in the U.S.S.R.," pp. 34–35.

24. Richard F. Nyrop, ed., *Israel: A Country Study* (Washington, D.C.: American University, 1979), p. 305.

25. Ibid., p. 60.

26. Samuel Rolbant, *The Israeli Soldier: Profile of an Army* (Cranbury, N.J.: Thomas Yoseloff, 1970), p. 228.

27. Nyrop, *Israel*, p. xx.

28. Charles C. Moskos, Jr., "The American Combat Soldier in Vietnam," *Journal of Social Issues* 31 (1975), p. 27.

29. Morris Janowitz, Letter, February 22, 1983.

30. Reuven Gal, "Unit Morale: Some Observations on Its Israeli Version" (Washington, D.C.: Department of Military Psychiatry, Division of Neuropsychiatry, Walter Reed Army Institute of Research, 1983), pp. 12–14.

11

Commitment in the Military: The Army Reserve Case

Thomas C. Wyatt

The general concept of commitment is reviewed in this chapter; the fit of that concept to the military setting is examined; and a study of how military commitment was measured empirically is reported.

Organizational factors more than individual factors increase membership commitment in U.S. Army Reserve units. In terms of military commitment, the individual's orientation to the organization is due to the organization. This conclusion was reached as a result of research which examined the membership commitment of individuals to U.S. Army Reserve organizations. Perhaps the most important outcomes of the effort reported here were that it is possible to measure commitment in the military and that a measurement methodology was developed.

There are few surprises to be found in this reported research when the findings are viewed from a military perspective. Military culture tends to suppress individualism, except at the very senior levels of command. The organization is held to be more important than its individual members. Sacrifices of self and friendships are expected of the members.

The available literature reporting commitment in organizations does not hypothesize underlying variables that might contribute to a concept of commitment. The interesting assessment is that although we can describe commitment to the military, we are, as yet, unable to explain much of the concept. Perhaps this is because much of organization theory is framed by the perspective of voluntary association. Military settings invite further examination because military organizations are not totally voluntary associations. For example, members are not free to leave the organization, or the work place, once they have joined. This work, therefore, is important to that body of theory.

COMMITMENT

Informed sources characterize organizational commitment as an attitudinal bonding of the member to the organization. It is seen as a condition of seeking to continue membership, and it is also indicated by willingness to perform extra or hazardous duty with that organization. The details of commitment are not well understood. Little explanatory research has been undertaken to add to our understanding of this social phenomenon; what we do know can be synopsized as follows.

Work in this area, dating at least to the turn of the century, has focused more on job satisfaction, morale, job attitudes, productivity, worker characteristics, work environment, management practices and leadership, motivation, and, especially, alienation. Commitment, on the other hand, has received little attention; most scientists and managers—both military and non-military—take it for granted.

Commitment is often the property of a social system and is not measured by a single individual attitude; the higher the status and the greater the involvement in the organization, the greater is the degree of commitment. Furthermore, commitment to an organization is also viewed as a function of the prestige of the organization and is indicated by friendship groups within the organization. While job satisfaction and commitment are not the same thing, commitment is usually found among those who place a high value on the intrinsic values offered by the job.

Personal success in the organization appears to increase commitment, whereas failure lowers it. Major influences on organizational commitment arise from personal, job, and organizational characteristics.

Retention and reenlistment in an organization appear to be indicators of commitment. This implies that the behavioral criterion of minimal commitment would be continuance in a role while engaging in as much covert and overt role distance as the individual or group can tolerate. Several citations in the research literature report a relationship between turnover and commitment to the organization. Personnel turnover in the military setting is indicated by reenlistments; retention and reenlistment are indicators of commitment in military organizations, suggesting that commitment is heavily influenced by perceptions of military life.

D. J. Champion, a groundbreaker in commitment research, devised the following analogy for organizational commitment: "Commitment is to a large organization as incentives are to work group and motivation is to an individual."[1] Organization and institution influences on the development of commitment have been reported. Onlookers (organization context) play an important part in the commitment process. An opinion or resolution or act made in private can be changed more easily than one made in public. In a similar vein, one cannot revoke a previous act and, therefore, one feels committed. Private commitment is more perishable than public acts associated with commitment, for example, reenlistments in the military. When personal factors, role-related factors, and organizational commitment are examined, a relationship is found to exist. It can be argued that the explanation of commitment should consider personal and organizational factors.

Previous research findings reported in the literature are summarized in the following statements:

- Commitment is the property of a social system and is not measured by a single individual attitude.
- The higher the organizational status the greater the involvement, hence the greater the commitment.
- Commitment to an organization is also a function of the prestige of that organization and may be indicated by friendship groups within that organization.
- Commitment is usually found among those who place a high value on the intrinsic values offered by the job.

- There is little relationship between job satisfaction and performance, but positive attitudes and work involvement have long range effects on turnover rates, absenteeism, and accidents.
- Commitment is that state where one is not free to break out of a bond even if there are negative feelings about that bond.
- Commitment is to a large organization as incentives are to a work group and personal motivation is to an individual.
- Commitment is present in those workers who identify with organizational goals.
- Public acts or statements create or increase the degree of commitment.
- When a person cannot revoke a public act, he is committed.
- When one is committed to the task, the task is usually seen as enjoyable and production increases.
- In order to be committed, one must feel bound and also must feel one has some choice in his or her actions.
- Those who make public commitments tend to become more extreme in their commitment.
- Acts of commitment observed by others tend to "freeze" the attitude of the actor.
- High participation is related to low alienation.
- Personal success in an organization increases commitment and feeling of competence; experiencing failure lowers job involvement.
- Highly competitive jobs are associated with high turnover rates and low commitment.
- Workers who respond to a high recruiting effort and join a particular organization have early high commitment. Procedures for maintenance of this high commitment are generally unknown.
- Staying on the job does not mean one is committed to it.
- When employees agree with organizational objectives, high commitment is usually present; commitment may be present in an organization where the worker is provided tasks with intrinsic value and where the worker can share in the decision making.

One is easily led to the conclusion that the military and civilian literature fails to disclose any systematic development of an understanding of commitment. Most of the research has been aimed at that to which a person is committed. Little information is available to suggest how an organization facilitates or maintains commitment. Commitment viewed as an attitudinal bonding is best understood in its various social settings (commitment to a particular person, to an organization, to an ideal, and so forth). Commitment may be indicated by behavior taken by the actor consistent with the attitude or by the report of this attitude.

COMMITMENT AND THE MILITARY—THE SUBJECT RESEARCH

E.A. Shils and M. Janowitz appear to have been first with the concept of organizational commitment in the military.[2] Forty years ago, according to Shils and Janowitz, organizational commitment was believed to be the positive end of the dimension of involvement (alienation was the other pole). Despite its age and obvious lack of development beyond the level of an axiomatic statement, that concept is virtually unchallenged today. Others have addressed organizational commitment in their studies of other aspects of the military but have never focused on it; instead, the orientation has been toward the individual, and the situation or organizational context has not been considered.

High commitment could be indicated by a "last ditch stand" in an apparently hopeless defensive situation. Alienation, the opposite of commitment and not merely a lack of commitment, could be indicated in the same situation by a unit or a person throwing away weapons and deserting.

When we consider the military case and commitment, we find a near ideal research platform; that is, the subject phenomenon is present and visible, the need to understand the subject is widely recognized, and previous attempts at explanation have been less than successful. We can conclude that among the large, formal, complex organizations of which we are aware, one that stands in great need of understanding organizational commitment is the military. Little is known of organizational commitment in or out of the military; less is known when we consider the context of the organization; and probably less still is known when the phenomenon is applied to the military reserves.

The generalizability of these findings is limited by several considerations. First, this research was exploratory and opportunistic; that is to say, it was piggybacked onto ongoing research, and it used secondary analysis of survey data collected for a different purpose. Second, it addressed a subset of the military subculture, the U.S. Army Reserves. Although this sample was statistically representative of that population, application to the entire military population would be risky, and extension to non-military sectors would be done at even a greater risk. Also, the U.S. Army Reserves are not clearly distinguishable as either voluntary or nonvoluntary associations or organizations in the conscription-free society of today. It would be difficult to apply these findings with more emphasis on one group or the other.

Another limitation of the contribution of the research findings to the general theory of organizations occurs not because of measurement or sampling error, but because of the uncertainty of the fit of military into our major culture. Further masking of our understanding of how what we know about commitment in the military generalizes to the larger society occurs because the military is not generally considered to be a dominant social force. Perhaps this is an error. The military does exercise influence on the shaping of our society because of its size, its sources of membership, and its uninterrupted tenure as a social institution. Most researchers fail to attend to the military subculture except during periods of war or threat of war. We would call this the Tommy Atkins syndrome, recalling Rudyard Kipling, "For it's Tommy this, Tommy that, and Tommy get behind; but it's 'Thank you Mr. Atkins,' when the troops are on the line."[3]

The analyses in this study leave little doubt that organizational properties are central to producing membership commitment, but the details of the process must be identified and examined more clearly now that we know where to look for explanations for this important social decision making. Organization theory does not yet explain the wide range of employee commitment; it does not examine the dynamics of employer-employee code-terminants of commitment; and the possible preconditions to commitment in the organization and the potential member are not found in the literature. Also in need of further study relevant to commitment is the correspondence between voluntary and nonvoluntary associations and organizations. And, finally, longitudinal studies of the commitment process as we can know it are required before casual effects of the organization on the members' commitment decision can be stated.

If organizations can be viewed as systems, if the military can be seen as a social system not unlike the society that supports it, and if organizational commitment is a social bonding of individuals to organizations, it can be argued that variations in social factors of military organizations will result in different levels of commitment of the membership. Certain social factors of organizations influence individual commitment to the organization more than do individual factors.

The reserve components of the military are larger than the active duty forces. This fact surprises most people, even military people. Reservists make up about 65 percent of the service support required for the active duty forces, 85 percent of its total medical support, and over 50 percent of the combat elements of the total force. A breakout of the total force is shown in Figure 11.1. Strategic plans call for the deployment of reserves as organizations and as individuals to reinforce the active duty forces in time of war. It is planned that reserves will rapidly assume the largest part of future war operations, as has been the historical case, except its senior leadership, which also has been the case.

Military reservists are neither full-time soldiers nor all-time civilians; also, the organizations of the military reserves today are neither clearly voluntary nor nonvoluntary, and they do not fit the traditional militia mold because of the mix of full-time and part-time members. Today, about one out of every ten reservists assigned to units is a full-time active-duty soldier. The proportion is more than double that number if it is an aviation organization. The days of the old familiar "weekend warrior" are a thing of the past.

The reserve components, then, may be a better representation of the general society than the active-duty force; consequently, understanding commitment in the military could best be begun with the reserves.

In the research reported here, nearly 1,000 members of army reserve, company-size units responded to survey and nonsurvey data collection in various locations across the United States. Differences in level of commitment among company-size organi-

Figure 11.1
Relationships of Total Force Components

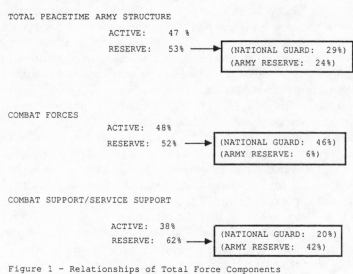

Figure 1 - Relationships of Total Force Components

Source: National Guard Association of the United States

zations were analyzed, and a comparison was made between organizational properties and individual factors as they influence commitment. This research explored a new way to look at commitment in a military setting because of the use of contextual analysis in the explanation of commitment; that is, it assessed the interaction of organizational factors and individual factors as they affected commitment in the setting where the process was taking place.

For the purposes of this research, organizational commitment in a U.S. Army Reserve military setting was defined as:

A condition of seeking to continue membership in a military organization. This may be indicated by reported intention to rejoin that organization prior to the expiration of the term of membership, or demonstrated by rejoining prior to the expiration of the term of membership; also, the act or reported intention of volunteering for hazardous duty or extra duty with the member's unit or similar organizations.

Figure 11.2
Regions of Commitment Strain

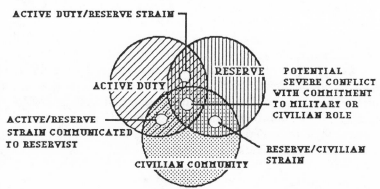

Further, commitment is facilitated or suppressed by the context of the organization of which the individual is a member.

This definition was constructed as a result of nearly three years of study and research of army reserve organizations and individuals. During this work, the condition of role strain affecting commitment was observed, as shown in Figure 11.2.

RESEARCH METHODS

Commitment may be seen as both an independent variable and a dependent variable; that is, commitment may be the cause of an effect and, also, the effect of some cause. For example, commitment is related to motivation, which is related to organizational effectiveness. An effective organization attracts people to it who are willing to commit to organizational goals. The research design considered this view.

The design was to use some form of attitude or behavior assessment to determine the direction of an individual's commitment to the military reserve organization of which that individual was a member. The unit of analysis was to be the individual. The dependent variable was organizational commitment, as defined above.

Independent variables suspected to be of some influence on the dependent variable were divided into two categories: individual and organizational. Although there was some interest in determining which personal characteristics affected commitment, the greatest interest was turned toward organizational characteristics that influenced individual commitment. One of the assumptions of this design was that something could be learned about organizational influence on individual commitment if commitment levels varied across organizations. Differences in individual commitment across units should result from differences in the organizational context, assuming no individual differences were found.

Research design, then, would consider the influence of one organizational level independent variable, voluntarism, and one individual level independent variable, stability, on the individual level dependent variable commitment. The individual commitment of members of army reserve units would be examined in the context of members' military units in order to determine if any organizational characteristics influenced the members' commitment.

Stability and voluntarism in an organization setting are discussed by Theodore Caplow as two criteria of organizational performance found throughout the literature of modern organization theory.[4] They have been guiding principles for more than three decades:

Stability is an organization's ability to maintain its own structure. In peacetime military organization, stability can be roughly measured by the tendency to reenlist. Voluntarism is an organization's ability to maintain the appropriate relationships among its positions and among its component units with a minimum of coercion. In a military setting, voluntarism includes morale in the classic sense, and can be roughly measured by the disposition to volunteer for hazardous duty.[5]

Stability has as its central theme, loyalty. Indiscipline is seen as a repudiation of membership and organizational commitment. Organizational spirit and pride are values which indicate voluntarism and, therefore, attachment to the organization.

Four instruments were used to collect the data: (1) a precoded questionnaire administered as a group interview to all unit officers and enlisted personnel at each of the selected field sites; (2) a more extensive interview form for administration to each commanding officer and executive officer of each unit in the sample; (3) a structure report format for use by field observers to record observations covering nine types of company activity (e.g., dining, recreation, training) to be observed at each of the sample sites; and (4) individual observation summaries to record the remarks of each of the field observers.

The three analysis techniques used are briefly described below.

1. Factor Analysis. This statistical technique was used to create a set of variables to represent a hypothetical variable. For example, theory suggested certain variables would be associated with the concept of organizational commitment. Factor analysis examined the interrelationships among these suggested variables and identified those variables that were consistent with the theory and reflected organizational commitment and those that were ambiguous and could be dropped from further consideration. A principal components program was run to look at the linear combination of the suggested variables. Orthogonal rotation looked for a simple structure of the concept of commitment. Two- and four-factor restrictions were called, and in each case five variables loaded on one factor and appeared to define commitment. These variables are described below. The same procedure defined the concepts of stability and voluntarism.

2. Multiple Regression. This statistical technique was used in this case to analyze the relationship between the variables identified in the factor analysis routines and, also, to examine the relationship between the independent variables, stability and voluntarism, and the dependent variable, commitment. Multiple regression was used to develop the structure of these variable relationships and to control alternately the effects of one independent variable while examining the influence of the other independent variable on the dependent variable. The impact of stability and voluntarism on commitment was thus determined. Multiple regression was used in the contextual analysis described below.

3. Contextual Analysis. Contextual analysis asks the question: "Is an individual's response affected more by one of his own traits or more by a characteristic of the group of which he is a

member?" Contextual analysis is used to establish boundaries of homogeneity of a social group. Contextual analysis also focuses on the individual but in reference to the group context. Contextual analysis examined the ways in which relationships between variables change systematically for individuals across groups set up to differ systematically on a group level variable. For example, we looked at relationships between individuals' values of reenlistment and commitment to determine systematic changes in their relationships across groups (units), differing by values of voluntarism. This analysis measured individuals on variables reflecting individual characteristics as well as a selected aspect of the group in which that individual was a member.

Recall that, in this study of military commitment, three variables were created—organizational commitment, voluntarism, and stability. Two independent variables—voluntarism and stability—were constructed by recoding selected variables from the original data collected from nearly 1,000 army reservists. Components of this new dependent variable, *commitment*, found in the original data are as follows:

Satisfaction with pay
Satisfaction with duty assignment
Incentive to do good work
Care about organization
Want to get out

The independent variable, *stability*, defined earlier as a desire to maintain membership, was created using the following variables:

Intention to reenlist
Rating of unit war readiness
Rating of unit equipment
Rating of unit training
Rating of unit officers
Rating of unit noncommissioned officers
Rating of unit enlisted personnel

The independent variable, *voluntarism*, defined earlier as volunteering intention and roughly equivalent to morale, was created using the following variables:

Assessment of unit effectiveness

Unit spirit

Intention to volunteer

Unit teamwork

Individual factors contribute very little to the concepts of commitment, stability, and voluntarism in U.S. Army Reserve company-size units. However, membership commitment to these organizations is significantly influenced by the context of the organizational setting in which the membership works.

This research did not attempt to establish casual relationships among the control variables at the individual or organizational levels. Instead, only those variables with significant direct effect on the defined concepts of commitment, stability, and voluntarism were of interest. Multiple regression analysis was used to select the variables to be examined and identified those variables that were not significant to the concepts and were subsequently eliminated.

For commitment, satisfaction with one's duty assignment had the highest weight, followed by perceived chances for promotion and satisfaction with pay. Nearly 60 percent of the common variance is explained by these components of commitment. Stability is defined by three respondent ratings. These are, in their weighted order, war readiness, unit training, and quality of unit officers. Over 70 percent of the common variance is accounted for by these components. Voluntarism comprises team spirit, weighted highest; teamwork within the unit, next; and, pride in the unit contributing, but with the least weight (see Table 11.1).

Variables in the present data which were suggested by the literature to be associated with the concept of commitment were as follows:

Training

Retirement benefits

Table 11.1
**Factor Loadings for Factors Derived from Factor Analyses of Data
on Organizational Commitment in the U.S. Army Reserves**

Factor	Variables	Factor Loadings	Eigen-value	Percentage of Variance
Commitment	Pay satisfaction	.339	1.292	59.2
	Duty satisfaction	.696		
	Promotion chances	.426		
Stability	Rate war readiness	.627	1.579	71.2
	Rate unit training	.613		
	Rate unit officers	.457		
Voluntarism	Pride in unit	.452	1.194	100.0
	Team spirit	.713		
	Teamwork	.693		

*   Principal component factor analysis with varimix ortho-
     gonal rotation; .333 is the cutoff for inclusion of a
     variable in a factor.

Extra income

Unit rating (overall evaluation)

Pay

Duty assignment

Chance for promotion

Work motivation

Care about the unit

Desire to end membership

For stability, the following variables were found:

Reenlistment intention

Unit war readiness

Unit equipment

Unit training

Table 11.2
Results of Regression of Commitment on Voluntarism and Stability for U.S. Army Reservists

Dependent Variable		Voluntarism	Stability	R2	F
Commitment	B	.7018	.2912	.1627	85.1907*
	s.e.	.0267	.0289		
	beta	.0917	.3523		

* Significant at p < .001

Unit officers
Unit sergeants and corporals
Unit other ranks (privates)

For voluntarism, the following variables were found:

Pride in unit
Unit team spirit
Volunteering intention
Unit teamwork

Of the total variance occurring when all the variables associated with commitment are exercising simultaneous influence, 60 percent of the variance is explained by a particular cluster of these variables. In the case of commitment, the variables were pay satisfaction, duty satisfaction, and chances for promotion. For stability, they were unit war readiness, unit training, and unit officer fitness. Voluntarism's variables were unit pride, unit spirit, and unit teamwork.

The contributions of stability and voluntarism to commitment were then assessed, using multiple regression analysis (see Table 11.2). Influence on commitment by stability is nearly four times larger than the influence by voluntarism. Analysis to this point showed a different level of individual member commitment among the sample organizations. What remained to be done was to look at individual factors and organizational properties to determine what, if anything, was contributing to this variation in the level of commitment.

Variables not included in the commitment, stability, and voluntarism equation were categorized as individual level or organizational level variables. These variables were submitted to multiple regression analysis to examine the structure of contextual influences. One individual level variable, sex, traditionally expected to appear in data analysis is not included here.

Individual level control variables do contribute to the development of organizational commitment but explain less than 4 percent of commitment (see Table 11.3). Age at enlistment records the highest coefficient and is in contrast with present age, which has negative value. Family status of members with a family including children shows the second highest value among the individual level factors. Nevertheless, these individual factors do not appear to explain much about commitment. Individual level factors are similarly weak contributors to stability and voluntarism. In the case of stability, less than 1 percent of the variance is explained by this set of variables, and little more than 2 percent of voluntarism is accounted for by these individual factors. The influence of the individual level variables on these components of commitment is not significant.

Organizational level variables tell a very different story (see Table 11.4). Organizational properties account for 24 percent of commitment, 44 percent of stability, and 20 percent of voluntarism. Also, this influence is statistically significant. As for commitment, satisfaction with weekend drill is considered to be the most important factor. Excepting two variables related to identification with the unit, good outfit and care about the unit, which also weigh heavily, other variable coefficients are nearly equal. A third exception, friendship networks, ranks close to drill satisfaction. The negative loading variable, which is the highest, is the rating of unit equipment. The magnitude and direction of this coefficient was expected, for reservists have traditionally made an issue of the fact that they receive used and well-worn items of equipment, handed down from active-duty forces. It would appear that the organizational climate of satis-

Table 11.3
Regression of Commitment, Stability, and Voluntarism on
Individual Level Control Variables for U.S. Army Reservists

Independent Variables	B	s.e.	beta	R2	F
Commitment					
A. Family status (with children)	.6330	.0373	.0103	.0451	3.0046*
B. Enlistment age	-.1166	.0578	-.1252		
C. Present age	.2184	.0738	.1642		
D. Race	.5718	.1146	.0031		
Stability					
A. Family status (with children)	.3834	.1170	.0021	.0090	.5837**
B. Enlistment age	.1172	.0381	.0189		
C. Present age	-.2762	.2219	-.0540		
D. Race	.1059	.0753	.0794		
Voluntarism					
A. Family status (with children)	-.5238	.1183	-.0275	.0239	1.5539**
B. Enlistment age	.1709	.0385	.0271		
C. Present age	-.1035	.0597	-.1089		
D. Race	.1458	.0762	.1073		

*   Significant at p < .05
** Not significant

fying weekend drills, good training, association with friends at the work place, and identification with the group are all operating here. This is consistent with the theory of organizations.

Organization level variables explain more of the concept of stability than they do commitment. Usefulness of training and satisfaction with weekend drills are working here, also, but they are stronger contributors to stability than they are to commitment. In the military culture, training is seen as one of the most important factors for success in combat, and combat is the ul-

Table 11.4
Regression of Commitment, Stability, and Voluntarism on Organization Level Control Variables for U.S. Army Reservists

Independent Variables	B	s.e.	beta	R2	F
Commitment					
A. Good outfit	.2026	.0914	.1170	.2366	10.81*
B. Training useful	.1192	.0541	.1131		
C. Training as expected	.1584	.0654	.1341		
D. Trained for job	.1036	.0419	.1241		
E. Weekend drill	.2744	.0775	.1893		
F. Unit Equipment	-.6107	.0818	-.0381		
G. Friends in unit	.2860	.0263	.0549		
H. Do my best	.1186	.0536	.1152		
I. Care about unit	.2017	.0665	.1544		
Stability					
A. Good outfit	.2103	.0781	.1211	.4445	27.92*
B. Training useful	.9936	.0462	.0941		
C. Training as expected	.2665	.0559	.2253		
D. Trained for job	.1164	.0358	.1392		
E. Weekend drill	.4509	.0663	.3104		
F. Unit Equipment	.2777	.0699	.1727		
G. Friends in unit	-.5016	.0225	-.0961		
H. Do my best	.1075	.0458	.1042		
I. Care about unit	.1330	.0568	.1016		
Voluntarism					
A. Good outfit	.1729	.0956	.0977	.1998	8.71*
B. Training useful	-.5088	.0565	-.0473		
C. Training as expected	.2315	.0684	.1920		
D. Trained for job	.9975	.0438	.1170		
E. Weekend drill	.1804	.0810	.1219		
F. Unit Equipment	.6438	.0855	.0393		
G. Friends in unit	-.4567	.0275	-.0859		
H. Do my best	.7955	.0560	.0757		
I. Care about unit	.2640	.0695	.1979		

* Significant at $p < .05$

timate test of productivity; and, also, effectiveness is not be based on friendships. Therefore, these findings are no surprise. Being trained for the current job and having the tools to do the work will encourage a member to do his best work in the organization. This is reflected by the highest coefficients among these variables. Also, if one is already trained for one's job, additional training detracts from one's willingness to make extra efforts for the organization; one seeks to do things in one's own interest rather than things in the interest of the organization. The negative value shown for friendship networks is not consistent with a sense of camaraderie, usually associated with morale, as part of the manifestation of voluntarism in a military setting.

CONCLUSIONS

The theoretical proposition that membership commitment in U.S. Army Reserve company-size units is influenced more by organizational properties than by individual factors is supported by the data. Furthermore, the concepts of stability and voluntarism prove to be constituents of organizational commitment and are similarly affected by organizational and individual factors.

More than that, this study has put forward a new way of describing a member's organizational commitment—a contextual frame of reference. This assessment is not new to social analysis or even to assessments of organizations; however, the examination of the individual's commitment to membership from the organization's perspective is new.

NOTES

1. D. J. Champion, *The Sociology of Organizations* (New York: McGraw-Hill, 1975).

2. E.A. Shils and M. Janowitz, "Cohesion and Disintegration in the Wehrmact in World War II," *Public Opinion Quarterly* 12 (1948), pp. 280–315.

3. R. Kipling, *Ballads and Barrack-Room Ballads* (New York: Doubleday, 1907).

4. Theodore Caplow, *Principles of Organizations* (New York: Harcourt, Brace and World, 1964).

5. Theodore Caplow, H. Bahr, and B. Chadwick, *Condition of the Army Reserves* (Washington, D.C.: Department of Defense, 1980).

Conclusion

In Part I of this volume, we discussed some theoretical issues of legitimacy and commitment in the military. The chapters in Part II identified selected sources of these concepts. Part III showed how legitimacy and commitment are manifest and measured in nations and organizations today.

A final word about legitimacy and commitment in the military is due, if only to add a social psychological dimension to these concepts.

Accepting that definitions are ultimately circular and that undefined and "primitive" terms are to be found in initial propositions in any inference system, we nevertheless attempt some summary definitions of legitimacy and commitment. We are offering a compressed description of these two subjects in order to invite additional consideration of them, realizing that the outcome will not satisfy all.

When certain power is socially recognized as acceptable, certain persons or groups of persons are empowered to act on behalf of society. Given this power by society, their actions are routinely accepted as appropriate; this assumed compliance by society members is voluntary. The voluntary compliance comes through an internalized (though a socialization process) understanding of society's normative code: the expectation to obey legitimate authority. The normative code is rationalized and enforced by the state—and its agencies—more than any other institution in our society. Furthermore, it has been said that we accede to authority demands because we are social beings; and when we accept the state's actions as legitimate, we also give over to the state some individual power—even though we may suffer from the consequences of its actions.

We recognize that legitimacy is a fuzzy concept until it is related to some other object; that is to say, one must ask, "Legitimacy of what?" In the chapters in this book, we have identified the military as the "what." We could define the military in several ways but prefer to consider it to be a social institution; therefore, when we view legitimacy, it is from the perspective of the compound concept of legitimacy and a social institution. The military is an institution with a definite, formal, and regular way of doing something. It is an established procedure.

Legitimacy in the military is achieved when the institution lives up to its members' expectations of competence and authority. Indeed, there are indicators of legitimacy in military institutions.

For our purposes, legitimacy in the military setting appears to have two dimensions of interest: value correspondence and legal-rational. The test of legitimacy would appear to reside in the degree of agreement with the procedures and purposes of institutional associations on the one hand (value correspondence) and agreement with the power and authority (legal-rational) on the other.

Indicators of legitimacy are of two kinds—value correspondence and legal-rational. Indicators of value correspondence are listed below:

- Recognition of competence among selected members of institutional associations
- Willingness to submit to dominance displayed by selected association policy or members
- Agreement with procedure and goals of institutional associations
- Willingness to participate in association activities
- Willingness to provide resources to associations of the institution

The indicators of legal-rational legitimacy are as follows:

- Recognition that an association of an institution has the legal power over association members
- Recognition of a superordinate-subordinate relationship in institutional associations
- Recognition that association authority does not extend beyond the boundaries of institutional associations
- Recognition that one is obliged to conform to the behavior expectations of associations of an institution

As for commitment, perhaps the most important consideration is that commitment is a two-way street, usually full of ideological and policy potholes; getting it smooth is difficult; and, if left unattended, it could seriously damage the system it supports.

Commitment is the process outcome of bonding together the individual and the organization—putting together the individual and the organization into a whole. Each shares common values with the other. There is a psychological contract operating in which the organization and the individual agree to exchange certain benefits and support for services and loyalty. The organization provides various forms of compensation, training, and the assets needed to perform work as well as occupational and personal support systems, including an efficient work environment, the proper tools, and a concern for individual welfare. In exchange, the individual becomes dedicated to and identified with the organization; the individual feels that he or she is making a contribution to the performance and reputation of the organization. Each party maintains a set of expectations of the other which are confirmed or denied by the behaviors of each. Leadership or management must identify and negotiate to satisfy the needs and expectations of the organization's members, creating the organizational environment that facilitates getting and keeping individual commitment, especially in today's military.

Four factors combine to construct the indicator of commitment in organizations—military or nonmilitary:

1. Membership Identifies with the Organization. First, the organization needs to know who it is. This means what it does, and did, and can do—where it fits in the scheme of things. Then

the organization members need to know who they are in that organization—where they fit in the scheme of things. The tricky part is setting the level of the organization with which you wish the membership to identify—and with which the membership wishes to identify and can identify.

2. A Sense of Professional Self-Satisfaction Is Present. This is a sense of doing well those things expected of a member of the organization—doing what is supposed to be done in support of the organization. When the work one is doing is seen by that person as helping the organization reach its goals, that member experiences a sense of contribution. This sense of contribution is not the direct result of evaluation feedback from superiors; rather, it is self-generated when the individual can realize an alignment of effort—his and that of the organization. This can lead to a sense of belonging on the part of the individual, and helps in internalizing organization values.

3. Pride in the Association of the Individual/Group and the Organization Is Present. This factor needs little explanation because its meaning is nearly primitive knowledge. When one takes pride in one's association with something, the tendency is to increase the strength of that association and attempt to maintain it. When we take pride in something we do we usually try to keep doing it. It feels good. We like to do things that feel good. If we see others who are proud of their association with something and see that they feel good about that relationship, it's not unlikely that we will want the same kind of association. Members of excellent organizations, or ones that seem to be excellent, are truly proud to be members. Those members of poor organizations do not boast of their membership, do not identify with it, and often try to leave.

4. Mutual Respect Exists. While this factor also needs little discussion, it is important to note that it illustrates the interdependency of the organization leadership and its members; each must hold the other in high regard, especially during times of stress and uncertainty. Mutual respect is most often earned, visible, and based on competence demonstrated by skillful performance of activities necessary to the success of the organization.

For those readers who may be uncomfortable with these descriptions of legitimacy and commitment in the military, we suggest that we have been considering the modern military environment—the one we have known since World War II and the one we may know in the near future.

Recommended Additional
Reading

Brown, James, and William Snyder, eds. *Defense Policy in the Reagan Years*. Washington, D.C.: National Defense University Press, 1988.

Caplow, Theodore. *Peace Games*. Middleton, Conn.: Wesleyan University Press, 1989.

Daft, Richard L. *Management*. New York: Dryden Press, 1988.

Galvin, General John R. *The Minute Men*. Washington, D.C.: Pergamon-Brassey, 1989.

Kohn, Stephen M. *Jailed for Peace*. Westport, Conn.: Greenwood Press, 1986.

Steers, Richard M., R.T. Mowday, and Lyman W. Porter. *Employee Commitment to Organizations: A Conceptual Review*, Technical Report No. 7. Eugene: University of Oregon, 1981.

Index

About the Contributors

Jere Cohen, Ph.D., is an associate professor of sociology at the University of Maryland, Baltimore County. His scholarship has encompassed both theory and research. The theoretical work has analyzed and tested classical sociological theories. A book currently in progress, *Max Weber and English Puritanism*, reassesses the famous Protestant ethic thesis. He has researched adolescent friendships, peer groups, and subcultures, and has recently studied parents' influence on adolescents. His work on status attainment has examined the educational and occupational attainment of military veterans, and he is planning a study of women's career patterns for the near future. Cohen has been active in the American Sociological Association and the Southern Sociological Society as a member and as a session organizer for their annual meeting, and has acted as a referee for various sociological journals and book publishers, and has served on the editorial board of the *American Sociological Review*.

Charles A. Cotton, Ph.D., teaches organizational behavior in the School of Business at Queen's University in Kingston, Ontario, Canada, where he is chairman of management programs. A former infantry officer with the Canadian forces, he served as head of the military leadership and management at the Royal

Military College of Canada from 1980 to 1983 with the rank of lieutenant-colonel. He is an active writer and consultant in the fields of leadership, defense organization, changing military values, and applied personnel research. He has been active in the Inter-University Seminar on Armed Forces and Society since 1975.

Reuven Gal, Ph.D., previously chief psychologist of the Israeli Defense Force, has also served as a combat officer in an elite infantry unit in the IDF and actively participated in the Six-Day's War in 1967. He has taught at Haifa University in Israel, served as a visiting professor in military education at Boston University, and has served as a National Academy of Science research associate at Walter Reed Army Institute of Research. Gal has published numerous articles on military psychology, behavior under stress, heroism in combat, and related subjects. His book *A Portrait of the Israeli Soldier* was published by Greenwood Press in 1986.

Wm. Darryl Henderson, Ph.D., Colonel (Ret) USA, received his doctorate in comparative political systems and international relations from the University of Pittsburgh. He has served as assistant professor and instructor in international relations, comparative systems, and military psychology at the United States Military Academy, West Point. He is a graduate of the Army's Command and General Staff College and the National War College where he was also a senior research fellow. His publications include *Cohesion: The Human Element in Combat* and *Why the Viet Cong Fought: A Study of Motivation and Control in a Modern Army in Combat*. He was coauthor and regional editor of *Handbook of World Conflicts*.

Donald L. Lang, Ph.D., is a lieutenant-commander in the Canadian Armed Forces, and serves in the capacity of advisor on matters of behavioral science. He also holds graduate degrees in psychology and educational administration. He is the editor of two international symposium reports on leadership: "Leadership for the 1990's" and "Commitment in the Military Profession." He taught psychology at Canadian military colleges for seven years, was a visiting professor at the University of Victoria, and currently teaches organizational psychology at the University of Ottawa.

Hillel Levine, Ph.D., received the rabbinic ordination from the Jewish Theological Seminary. From 1973 to 1980 he taught sociology and Jewish history at Yale University, where he founded the program in Judaic studies. He is currently professor of sociology and religion at Boston University and director of its center for Judaic Studies. He directs the Washington Internship on Community and Polity to train advocates for the Jewish community and for not-for-profit organizations. In 1989 he taught Jewish history at the Chinese Academy of Social Sciences and several universities in the People's Republic of China. He is the author of several studies in sociology and Jewish history.

Frederick J. Manning, Ph.D., is currently the director of the Division of Neuropsychiatry at the Walter Reed Army Institute of Research. In this role, he leads a multidisciplinary team of fifty military and civilian scientists in exploring the causes, mechanisms, and consequences of combat stress. A lieutenant colonel in the U.S. Army, he has published more than fifty journal articles and book chapters on a wide range of topics from neuroscience and behavioral pharmacology to the social psychology and culture of army life.

David H. Marlowe, Ph.D., currently chief of the Department of Military Psychiatry at the Walter Reed Army Institute of Research, began a long and distinguished career in military medical research studying the stress of basic training even before he earned his doctorate in social anthropology from Harvard University in 1963. He studied transcultural issues in Thailand and Vietnam in the mid 1960s before returning to Washington, D.C., and focusing on the social and organizational aspects of performance under stress. Marlowe also holds appointments in preventive medicine and psychiatry at the Uniformed Services University of the Health Sciences.

Charles Moskos is professor of sociology at Northwestern University and chairman of the Inter-University Seminar on Armed

Forces and Society. Moskos has been a Fellow at the Woodrow Wilson International Center for Scholars and the S.L.A. Marshall Research Chair at the Army Research Institute. His writings in military sociology have been translated into eight languages.

David R. Segal, Ph.D., is a professor of sociology and of government and politics at the University of Maryland, College Park. He spent the 1988–1989 academic year as visiting professor of sociology at the United States Military Academy, West Point. Among his books are *Recruiting for Uncle Sam, Life in the Rank and File, The All-Volunteer Force,* and *The Social Psychology of Military Service.* Segal is a member of the board of directors of the Inter-University Seminar on Armed Forces and Society, vice president of the Research Committee on Armed Forces and Conflict Resolution of the International Sociological Association, and a member of the council of the Section on Peace and War of the American Sociological Association. From 1982 to 1988 he served as editor of the quarterly journal, *Armed Forces of Society.* Among his other activities, he is a guest scientist in the Department of Military Psychiatry, Walter Reed Army Institute of Research, and a staff consultant to the National Security and International Affairs Division, U.S. General Accounting Office.

Eugene Weiner, Ph.D., is a faculty member of the Haifa University Department of Sociology. He has served as Chairman of the Department and is presently in charge of Graduate Studies. He is a graduate of Columbia College, The Jewish Theological Seminary and Columbia University. He has lived in Israel for the past 21 years. He served as a Captain in the Israel Defense Forces (Reserve) and saw duty in the Yom Kippur and Lebanon Wars in the Behavioral Sciences Division of the I.D.F. He is author with Anita Weiner of *Israel: A Precarious Sanctuary* (1989), *Expanding the Options in Child Placement: Israel's Dependent Children in Care from Infancy to Adulthood* (1990), and *The Martyr's Conviction: A Sociological Analysis* (1990).

Claude E. Welch, Jr., Ph.D., has been a professor of political science at the State University of New York at Buffalo since 1964. He has specialized in the academic study of armed forces in developing countries for over 20 years. Major books on this topic include *Soldier and State in Africa* (1970), *Military Role and Rule* (1974), *Civilian Control of the Military* (1976), *Anatomy of Rebellion* (1980), and *No Farewell to Arms?* (1987). He edits *Armed Forces & Society*, the quarterly journal of the Inter-University Seminar on Armed Forces and Society, and he is subject editor for the forthcoming *International Military and Defense Encyclopedia.*

Thomas C. Wyatt, Ph.D., began military service with the Iowa National Guard and went to war with 133d Infantry, 34th Division during World War II. He has served with U.S., British, and French forces in Europe, Korea, and Southeast Asia. In the public sector, Wyatt has served as consultant to the secretary of defense for reserve affairs. In the private sector, he has designed and conducted scientific research on military matters for more than twenty years, much of which has been dedicated to the reserve components. As an academic, he has held faculty posts at the graduate and undergraduate levels at San Jose State University and George Mason University. He has been a Fulbright exchange professor in Bangkok, Thailand, and he taught at the U.S. Military Academy at West Point and the Navy's Post Graduate School in Monterey, California.